BORN IN 1940?
WHAT ELSE HAPPENED?

RON WILLIAMS

AUSTRALIAN SOCIAL HISTORY

BOOK 2 IN A SERIES OF 32

FROM 1939 to 1970

War Babies Years (1939 to 1945):   7 Titles

Baby Boom Years (1946 to 1960):   15 Titles

Post Boom Years (1961 to 1970):   10 Titles

BOOM, BOOM BABY, BOOM

PRELIMINARY MATTERS

Published by Boom Books
Wickham. NSW. Australia
Web: www.boombooks.biz
Email: email@boombooks.biz

© Ron Williams, 2013. This revised edition: 2020

A single chapter or part thereof may be copied and reproduced without permission, provided that the Author, Title, and Web Site are acknowledged.

Creator: Williams, Ron, 1934 - author
Title: Born in 1940 : what else happened? / Ron Williams.
Edition: Premier edition
ISBN: 9780648771609 (soft cover)

Some Letters used in this text may still be in copyright. Every reasonable effort has been made to locate the writers. If any persons or their estates can establish authorship, and want to discuss copyright, please contact the author at email@boombooks.biz

Cover images: National Archives of Australia C5487, PH/0370, soldier on Thursday Island; C123, 8408, Japanese wool buyer with locals; A11666, 42, nurses on the first transport; A6180, 18/3/77/21, Alf Tregear, inventor operating a pedal wireless.

CONTENTS

EVACUATION OF PUBLIC SERVANTS	2
BRITISH WAR ORPHANS	9
PUNCH-UPS IN SYDNEY'S DOMAIN	11
WHAT WERE PEOPLE AT HOME DOING?	17
FOR OWNERS OF DRAFT HORSES	26
JINGOISM IS GROWING	36
COMMUNISM IN AUSTRALIA	50
WAR ON THE WESTERN FRONT	57
ATTITUDES IN OZ	69
BRITS ON THEIR OWN	73
THE FALL OF FRANCE: A BRITISH VIEW	76
POSTPONE THE ELECTIONS	93
THE BATTLE HOTS UP	101
A DELAYED RESPONSE ON SHEEPSKINS	104
THE BLITZ OF LONDON	115
THE OZ FEDERAL ELECTION.	119
HITLER LOOKS ELSEWHERE	127
WHAT IS CONTEMPORARY ART?	137
WHAT'S ON IN GREYHOUND CIRCLES?	142
ITALY JOINS THE PARTY	143
THE MELBOURNE CUP	152
THE END OF A TOUGH YEAR	157
OZ POLITICS ON THE NOSE	160
SUMMING UP 1940 IN OZ	167

IMPORTANT PEOPLE AND EVENTS

King of England	George VI
Prime Minister of Oz	Robert Menzies
Leader of Opposition	John Curtin
Governor General	Lord Gowrie
The Pope	Pius XII
US President	Theodore Roosevelt
PM of Britain	Nev. Chamberlain
After May	Winston Churchill
Leader of Soviet Russia	Joseph Stalin
Emperor of Japan	Hirohito
Prime Minister of Japan	Ideti Tojo

MELBOURNE CUP WINNERS

1939	Rivette
1940	Old Rowley
1941	Skipton

THE ASHES

1938	Australia 1, England 1

From 1939 to 1946, cricket was suspended because of the war.

1946	Australia 3, England 0

ACADEMY AWARDS

Best Actor	James Stewart
Best Actress	Ginger Rodgers

INTRODUCTION TO THE SERIES

I was five years old when the War started. But even at that early age, I was aware of the dread, and yet excitement, that such an epoch-making event brought to my small coal-mining town. At the start, it was not at all certain that it would effect us at all, but quickly it became obvious that everybody in the nation would become seriously involved in it. The most immediate response I remember was that all the Mums (who still remembered WWI) were worried that their sons and husbands would be taken away and killed. After that, I can remember radio speeches given by Chamberlain, Churchill, Lyons, Menzies, and Curtin telling of hard times ahead, but promising certain victory over our wicked foes.

For a young boy, as the War years went on, reality and fantasy went hand in hand. As I heard of our victories, I day-dreamed of being at the head of our Military forces, throwing grenades and leading bayonet charges. I sank dozens of battleships from my submarine that was always under attack. And I lost count of the squadrons of Messerschmitts that I sent spiraling from the sky. Needless to say, I was awarded a lot of medals and, as I got a bit older, earned the plaudits of quite a few pretty girls.

But, mixed in with all this romance were some more analytical thoughts. Every day, once the battles got going, I would go to the newspapers' maps of where the battlelines currently were. One for the Western front, one in North Africa, and a third in Russia. Later, another in the Pacific. Then I would examine them minutely to see just how far we had moved, backwards or forwards. I read all the reports, true and false, and gloated when it was said we were winning, and shrunk away from our losses.

At the personal level, I remember the excitement of getting up at 4am on a few days when nearby Newcastle was under submarine attack. We went to our underground air-raid shelter that we shared with a neighbour, and listened, and occasionally looked out, for some who-knows-what enemies to appear. It really was a bit scary.

I can remember too the brown-outs, and the black-outs, the searchlights, the tank-traps, the clackers that were given to wardens to warn of gas attacks, and the gasmasks that 20 town-wardens (only) carried, presumably to save a town of 2,000 people when needed. Then there was the rationing, the shortages of everything, and even the very short shirt tails that a perceptive Government decreed were necessary to win the War.

At the start of researching this book, everything began to come back to me. Things such as those above, and locations like Dunkirk, Tobruk, El Alemain, Stalingrad, and Normandy. Really, at this stage these names kept popping up, but I was at loss as to how significant they were. Also, names of people. Hitler and Mussolini I knew were baddies. But how bad? Chamberlain was always criticised for his appeasement, but what were his alternatives? Who were Ribbentrop and Molotov, and Tojo and Blamey, and what was Vichy France?

And finally, when war did come, and grind on, year after year, what effect did it have back here in Australia? How did we as a society cope with a world that just had to continue on, given that the sons and dads of the nation were actually being killed daily overseas? When the postman did his normal delivery and brought a letter saying your loved one is dead? What did we do when old jobs suddenly disappeared, and new ones were created a hundred miles away? When goods, long readily available, were no longer for sale? When everything changed?

It was all a hotch-potch to me when I started this series. At the end of it, I can say it is a lot clearer. I have sorted out the countable things like battles, locations, people, and rules and regulations. I can appreciate, too, the effects on society, though these can only be ascertained from what I have researched, and make no allowance for all that I have missed.

In presenting each book, I have started every chapter with a visit to Europe, and a look at the military events in the world, with increasing emphasis on the Pacific. Then I come back to Oz to see how we are faring in a military sense. After that, I blunder about reporting and speculating on which aspects of life here were affected by these, and other ongoing, matters.

So, despite all the talk about the War above, and despite the fact that it was the controlling influence on all of our lives, the thrust of these books is about the social changes and reactions that took place in this period, here in Oz.

EUROPE'S LEGACY FROM EARLIER

As I see it, there are four major background stories you will need at the start of this book.

The first theme. Adolf Hitler had perceived that the Allies (Britain and France) would bend over backwards to avoid war. He wanted two things very strongly. **He wanted to claim the millions of Germans** who had been taken into the new nations that were created at the end of WW1. **And he wanted more "living space."** So, from 1938 until March 1939, he had taken control of Austria, Czechoslovakia, and then Poland. By then, it was apparent that he was quite happy to gradually take over all the small nations of Europe one after another, so the Allies said "enough is enough", and declared war.

The second theme. This war quickly degenerated into what was called a "**phoney war**." That was because the Allied Armies became holed up in the 400-mile set of fortifications along the German-French border, called the Maginot Line, and when winter set in, everyone closed up shop. So the armies sat there in their bunkers and played fan tan.

The Navy was not so lucky. Its ships, and those of the merchant marine, were under constant attack, particularly by submarines, from the very outbreak of war, and their losses were a great concern. The Royal Air Force, were testing their mettle and craft in sorties over Scotland and the Channel, though as the northern winter came, activity there was necessarily reduced. Importantly though, there were no air raids on London or elsewhere. Perhaps, thought the Brits, peace might somehow breakout at any time.

The third theme. By Christmas, the British people had now become used to blackouts, petrol rationing, carrying gasmasks, limited sporting fixtures and theatres, conscription of the menfolk, propaganda and restrictions on free speech, air raid shelters, and the like. Over **half a million schoolchildren had been evacuated from London** and the large cities, and sent to safe places in the country, though this well-executed manoeuvre was **beginning to reverse** as it seemed that cities would not be bombed.

The fourth theme. On the other side of Europe, Russia was getting belligerent. It had much peace of mind because in August 1939, **she had completed a non-aggression pact with Germany**. This told her that she could invade her neighbours near Germany without getting into strife with the German Nazis. So, when Poland was conquered, Russia got the eastern third of that nation. Then she applied threats and easily persuaded the small Baltic States of Latvia, Lithuania and Estonia to come and join the party. After that, the big Red bully wanted the Scandinavian country of Finland in the north, and by the New Year was bunkered down on her borders waiting for the end of winter.

AUSTRALIA'S LEGACY FROM EARLIER

In Australia, we declared War on Germany at the same time as England. Here in Oz, the War initially seemed remote, and the ARP, (Air Raid Precautions) carrying their gasmasks, were generally ridiculed as they went about checking black-outs and blowing whistles. As the year progressed, and the War in Europe got more serious, and places like Poland fell to the enemy, people started to take matters more seriously. The Government at last got its act together and laid the basis for a solid Army. Our first batch of airmen arrived in London in December 1939, and there they were feted.

The mood in Australia was cautious. Everyone with memories of **WWI** feared War. But it was hard to realise that it would happen to us again, especially given that the Phoney War was promising, maybe, that things would not be so bad.

SOME MORE BACKGROUND LETTERS

Comment. Throughout this book, I use **Letters to the various newspaper Editors** to illustrate news and views. They are mainly from the Sydney Morning Herald, (*SMH)*, the (Melbourne) *Argus*, the *Canberra Times*, and the *London Times*.

Letter, H Todd. I continue to be perplexed by the half-hearted calls to join the Services being made by our political leaders. They are adamant that this is a time of crisis, of national emergency, yet they go soft on calling for men to join up. They clearly want to be able to say "I told you so" if things get worse, but they are frightened of the **parent vote** that does not want their boys to go off to war.

As usual, these politicians are miles behind the people. The people have accepted that war is on our doorstep, and that men will be made to fight it. They do not need politicians sugar-coating this.

Letter, Sir Henry Gullett, Federal Minister for Communications. This Government takes the position that it is not by constant harping, or by fiery speeches, that we will recruit young men. We are happy to say we live in a free society where facts and news are freely available to all. We consider that the terrible happenings in Austria, Czechoslovakia, and Poland, and the terrible tragedies at sea, are enough to convince men to do whatever they can to help. When these young men are convinced of real danger, they will flock to the cause. We do not want them to come in because of someone's rhetoric, but because they truly believe they are needed.

Letter, Tom Burns. I appreciate the Minister's point of view. But it would be much easier to be patriotic, and to join up, if the Government had not spent all of last year making mistakes and then covering them up. I will not go into the long list of starts and re-starts that it went through, but will mention one supreme piece of extreme deception. Many of the men now in the Second AIF joined when there was a Government assurance that they would not have to serve overseas. **Now that guarantee has been withdrawn**, and the men are compelled to stay in service. There are dozens of such instances I can quote, and Gullett's fine words will not get his fine soldiers until they are all sorted out.

And what about the lists of Reserved Occupations for the few who were called up. They mean that anyone with a job can get out of service. I suggest he makes a realistic list as if there is a war brewing, and stop treating us as morons.

Composite Editorial. Today the men of the Second AIF will parade through the streets of Sydney. It is timely that they should make such a public appearance because, up till now, the military preparations that this country have been making have been shrouded in a secrecy and official obfuscation that has made these men almost invisible. That has meant that the patriotic fervour that we should be extolling is diminished to the point of being dubious.

For the second time within a generation, our men of all ages are being called to arms. **This time, with the advantage of our earlier experience, they are not going with false hopes of glamour and adventure.** Rather they go because they see it as their duty to defend our country and Empire from all the evils that totalitarianism, embodied in Nazism and Fascism, entail.

The original AIF, which fought so heroically in WWI, will stand as a grand example to this fine body of men. When the time comes, they will certainly prove to be of the same calibre. The torch has been handed on, and these men are ready to bear it. They offer to this country the most that any body of men can offer – their own lives. When called, they will leave here with the prayers and hopes for speedy return from every person in this grateful nation.

Comment. There was great reluctance to send our Army overseas. For our Air Force, for some reason, things were quite different. We had already landed some airmen in England, and more were now enlisting in an Empire force of considerable size, that was destined for service in Britain. Perhaps the difference was due to **WWI thinking.** In that war, the Army was of vital importance, and the Air Force just a side-show. Given that, it could be argued, we could send the airmen away, but **we needed to keep our Army here** where it might be needed. Few people fully realised how important the Air Force would be this time round.

Letters, A Reeves. The Finns cannot continue much longer without help in men, money, arms, and warm clothes. Their victory or defeat is as important to the civilised nations as to the Finns themselves, for our success depends largely upon their success in checking Russia. But a tiny nation of less than 4,000,000 cannot continue indefinitely the single-handed fight against the enormous Russian nation of more that 178,000,000.

A meeting is to be held next Thursday to raise help for Finland. I shall very gladly give 50 Pounds at once if nine others will agree to give the same amount. The quicker the better. We double our gifts by giving quickly.

Comment. This resistance from Finland was nothing short of heroic. It was inevitable that she would be conquered, yet she fought on. The whole world was watching and admiring, right through the depths of winter, but no country could and would come to her aid militarily. It was just too much to expect some outside nation to take on the Russian Bear for a country that most people had scarcely heard of. So, this poor country continued to fight alone, grinding its way to the inevitable defeat when winter thawed.

CONSCIENTIOUS OBJECTORS

In some places, feeling was running quite high. There was a small number of young men in the community who had a "conscientious objection" to war, meaning that they would not be prepared to train for military service. Most of them were prepared to serve in other capacities, but not in any role requiring active service.

The sixth annual Country Convention of our ruling United Australia Party voted, without the need for discussion, that such objectors be granted **no** exemptions or alternatives at all, and should do their military training in the same manner as all others.

Keep an eye on these as the War hots up.

MY RULES IN WRITING

Now we are just about ready to go. First, though, **I give you a few Rules I follow as I write**. They will help you understand where I am coming from.

Note. Throughout this book, I rely a lot on reproducing Letters from the newspapers. Whenever I do this, I put the text in a different font, and indent it a little, and make the font somewhat smaller. **I do not edit the text at all.** That is, I do not correct spelling or grammar, and if the text gets at all garbled, I do not correct it. It's just as it was seen in the Papers.

Second Note. The material for this book, when it comes from newspapers, is reported as it was seen at the time. If the benefit of hindsight over the years changes things, then I might record that in my Comments. **The info reported thus reflects matters as they were seen in 1970**.

Third Note. Let me also apologise in advance to anyone I might offend. In a work such as this, it is certain some people will think **I got some things wrong. I am sure that I did**, but please remember, all of this is only my opinion. And really, **my opinion does not matter one little bit in the scheme of things**. I hope you will say "silly old bugger", and shrug your shoulders, and **read on**.

JANUARY: THE WAR IN FINLAND

Britain at the New Year was torn between apprehension and hope. **She was apprehensive** because she had been living in the shadow of war for almost two years, and because her troops were now in France, in the comfort of the Maginot Line, waiting to do, or not do, battle with the Hun. She was also apprehensive because every day her airmen were fighting air-battles against the Germans over the North Sea, and Scotland, and her fine young men were dying as a result. Also because her ships were being sunk in worrying numbers by the submarines and mines of the enemy. The number so far killed in the War was less than the road toll, but everyone knew the situation could get much worse in a short time, and so the nation was apprehensive.

On the other hand, it was hopeful. After all, the War had appeared to be seriously under way when Poland was invaded, and Britain and France declared war. But neither country got involved in the fighting there, and though Poland disappeared from the maps of Europe, no war had actually come to Britain. Since then, her troops had gone to France to sit in the massive Maginot Line defences, but with only token fighting taking place in just a small part of the Line. So there was room for hope. **Perhaps**, despite what the politicians were saying, this break in hostilities signalled a lessening in the resolves to fight, and somehow peace would be garnered.

The only place where there was any **real land war was in Finland.** As I said earlier, the Russians there were in temporary retreat against the Finns. These latter were will-of-the-wisp fighters, on skis, who came and went with great speed and no noise. They fought very few battles, but ambushed, harassed, and then retreated on their skis into forests and swamps where Russian vehicles and tanks could not follow.

The problem was that when winter was over, and the ground hardened, the Russians would then be able to follow, and it looked likely that the valour of the Finns could not save them. It was an ominous sign that whenever weather permitted, hundreds of Russian planes would bomb the Finn cities, and the Finnish Air Force had no means left to defend them.

Within Britain, controversies from last year continued. **The evacuation of school children from the cities to the country was now being remorselessly reversed**, as more people thought that the cities might escape bombing altogether. Problems with blackouts, and sporting fixtures, and the closing of theatres were slowly being rationalised, and the **Letters to the Times** were showing a frivolity that had not been seen for months.

EVACUATION OF PUBLIC SERVANTS

Public Servants, however, now emerged as a group with a grievance. When War was declared, it was announced that the vast British Public Service would be dispersed, from London, to all parts of Britain. Now that the cities were not being bombed, the Public Servants, like the school children, wanted to come home.

> **News item, January 23rd.** The Staff Side (a Trade Union group) of the Whitley Council for the Civil Service is continuing its agitation against further evacuation of Civil Servants from London so long as present conditions continue. Request has been made to the Chancellor of the Exchequer for an opportunity to put before him

the view of the Staff Side, which is stated to be virtually unanimous.

It is being represented to Sir John Simon that transfer to the provinces at short notice for an indefinite period, and, indeed, without any assurance of return, is a hardship which in peace-time would be judged a very hard one. Complaint is made that the terms granted to Service personnel evacuated, and the conditions under which the evacuation has been carried out, add to the hardship. The efficient conduct of public business has been made more difficult, and so far there has been immunity from air attack.

Having failed to obtain, through channels open to them, an explanation of the present or potential advantages of the evacuation which would reconcile the staff to the hardships they suffer, the Staff Side wants to tell the Chancellor of the Exchequer why it thinks, in present circumstances, the evacuation should be abandoned. The Staff Side considers the matter to be of the highest importance from the two standpoints of the staff affected and of Government policy.

Comment. This **very civilised** news report hides a seething mass of discontent within the Public Service at the compulsory relocation of Departments to locations right round the nation. **In the first place**, as Mr Albury, of Folkestone observed "we had been working in great sandstone and granite edifices that bombs would bounce off. We had great cellars and basements that nothing could penetrate. We were in the safest places in England. And they moved us out to the flimsy mansions in the country."

In the second place, Departments were now scattered everywhere, and this meant great inefficiencies. And **in the third**, to some people it seemed that it was now time to return to London. Of course, the situation here was different from that of the school children, because the Civil Servants had been ordered en masse to the country, whereas the childrens' moves had been voluntary. So the children could dribble back over time, but the Civil Servants could go back only if their Departments went back. This was a growing mess that clearly had no easy solution, and an irritant that generally lasted for the full War.

RATIONING IN BRITAIN

In Britain, rationing of four commodities was about to start. This had been mooted for months, and the complaints had poured in, though these were equally balanced by expressions of understanding of the inevitability of it all. But there were all sorts of iniquities. One of these is expressed below.

> **Letters, J Mason, Green Meadows, Ley Hey Park, Marple.** One of the problems of rationing which has so far escaped mention in the national Press concerns those many thousands of unmarried people who are forced by reason of their work to live away from their relations. In innumerable cases they must take their midday meal, tea, and often supper in works canteens, in public-houses, and restaurants, at a considerable distance from the house where they lodge.

Under present transport conditions they start out for work before the shops open and return in the black-out after they have closed. They must carry their ration-book with them if they are to obtain meals during the day, and yet in some way their landlady or hostess requires their book slips at least twice each week (if fresh food is to be obtained and no refrigerating facilities are available) if she is to look after their breakfast arrangements. There is in many cases absolutely no possibility of their purchasing supplies for themselves owing to the location of their work (the great majority of the younger personnel in the engineering trades come under the category discussed and the lunch interval is hopelessly inadequate for shopping).

There seems to be no alternative but a voluntary restriction of their meat course, an anomaly which democracy and the Ministry must remove in some way. Otherwise their fitness will deteriorate while engaged on nationally important work, and they will be forced to return again to their family's home, with a consequent maladjustment of the labour market.

BREADMAKING SECRETS IN BRITAIN

Letters, M Berkeley, Haywards Heath. As a grateful customer, I would like to say there is also a mill at Lindfield, Sussex, where wheat is stoneground and bread made as God intended man to have it!

For many years I have used nothing else but stoneground bread. It is largely to this that I attribute my own, and in the past, my household's practical immunity to influenza, common colds, and the dozen other complaints which seem to seize the average Englishman from November to April. It is well known that the finest constitution will go down under malnutrition and that the worst form of malnutrition is bread, which, deprived of its essential qualities, is no longer the "staff of life," as its chief form of nutriment, but a prolific cause of gastric ulcers, a starved nervous system, and all the other spectres which haunt the steps of the man or woman suffering from under-nourishment. No other food, no matter the quantity, can take the place of bread, or rather (since bread nowadays may mean anything or, more likely, nothing) wheat.

How grand it would be if we could see the windmills at work again on the local harvest and every woman taught to make bread as a necessary part of her education. There is a whole apostolate here.

OZ MILITARY NEWS

John Curtin was leader of the Australian Labor Party, and also Leader of the Opposition. Over the last few months, he had made it clear that Labour policy was that our military forces should not serve overseas. Not even in the Pacific and South East Asia. His statements on this matter were under constant scrutiny.

Letters, Arthur Griffith. Mr Curtin's clear declaration to the effect that the Labor Party in Australia is solid with Britain and France in the war will be welcomed not alone in this country, but throughout the Empire. This bold declaration of policy alone however, is not sufficient. Unless

Mr Curtin desires that Australia should adopt the same role as the USA (i.e., merely that of a benevolent neutral, willing to sell its produce to the Allies) he will need to modify his statement of some months back that "not a soldier must leave Australia."

There may be some basis for opposing the sending of Australian troops to the European war zone, on the ground that Britain and France can supply all the man-power needed, but to refuse a request, should it be made, to supplement the garrisons of Singapore, and Aden, and Suez, would be without any sort of justification. The more intelligent members of the Australian Labour Party realise that Singapore in the hands of a hostile power, whether European or Asiatic, would mean within the not far distant future, the end of Australia.

Letters, Loyalist. I have just returned from a tour of Great Britain. Early in November of last year, while conversing with an influential London merchant, I was rather priding myself on Australian loyalty. My friend quietly but firmly replied, "Does it not pay you to be?" He further asked me, "Is it not true that some of your leading Labour politicians are advocating that not a soldier must leave Australia to fight for the Empire?" I replied that I understood that was so. My friend then asked, "What would happen if Britain adopted the same attitude and refused to give Australia the protection of the British fleet?" I replied, "Chaos."

Letters, F Keen. As an international message serving a purpose, the broadcast delivered by

Mr Curtin as to Labour's attitude to the war was admirable. But as this slumbering war is merging into a sterner reality, we in Australia desire and require a more definite and practical war policy from the leader of the Labour Party.

In November last, in the Sydney Town Hall, Mr Curtin elaborated his party's attitude to the war, in the course of which he stated, "We will not be a party to sending troops overseas." The test of a man's sincerity is to know how he would actually respond to a given set of circumstances. Supposing the given set of circumstances to be that of the present, and Labour in power, with Mr Curtin as Prime Minister, would he and his Cabinet refuse to send troops overseas to assist the Mother Country, from which we all sprang, in the Empire's crucial hour of need?

He also stated at the Town Hall meeting, "The Labour Party always has and always will stand for the adequate defence of Australia," yet during the voluntary recruiting campaign launched by Mr Hughes, not a single Labour leader appeared on any platform voicing to the young men of Australia the duty behoving them to fit themselves for the defence of their country. His statements are not consonant with his broadcast. Lip service deludes no one, not even Mr Curtin's own party members.

I write from no party political point of view, but to abjure Labour to contribute to a full, complete and united war policy honouring what Alfred Deakin so eloquently described our country as "A pearl set in the Southern Seas, the brightest gem in Empire's crown."

BRITISH WAR ORPHANS

Letters, E Mac. In the "Herald" of January 9 appears a reference to a project planned by an Australian organization for the adoption of British war orphans. In this country of bounteous fruit, meat, and vegetables, we have enough and to spare for all the orphans in the United Kingdom. It would not only be helping them to bring them here, but every primary producer would benefit. Orphanages in Britain are financed by charities, and usually their incomes are too meagre to allow of anything but the plainest of food; fruit is considered a luxury.

I would suggest that **all inmates of orphanages in Britain be transferred to Australia**, and that the support given them by charities be transferred with them. That support in sterling at the present rate of exchange would help to pay the passages of the children.

OZ NEWS AND VIEWS

As I have worked my way though 1939 and now into 1940, it became obvious that the Western World was getting more religious as the news got progressively worse. The newspapers were supplied with a growing number of Letters, the clergy were getting their Sunday sermons into the newspapers, Church attendances were rising, and even the troops were attending Sunday services in large numbers. This was true here in Australia, and equally true in Britain, as the following odd mix shows.

Letters, Rev G Henniker-Gotley, Vivelsfield Vicarage, Haywards Heath. During the Great War, daily at 3 pm, the hour when the Saviour offered His life for men, many remembered in mental prayer those of their fellow-men who were suffering or had given their lives for them. Might not this devotion be revived during 1940?

Letters, Tancred Borenius, Westminster. Referring to the Letter regarding the English Apostle of the Finns, which has recently been published in your columns, it is proper to note that the present week witnesses the recurrence of the Feast of the Saint, which falls on the 19th of January.

It is a matter of special gratification to the Finnish colony in England, and indeed to the whole of Finland that, after a lapse probably of many centuries, a special Votive Mass in honour of St Henry of Finland will be celebrated at Westminster Cathedral at 11.30am on St Henry's Day for the salvation of the Finnish people. The Bishop of Lamuswill pontificate and his Eminence the Cardinal Archbishop of Westminster will assist at the Mass.

Letters, Melville Gerry. To expect the world to run smoothly without reference to God is a vain hope. There cannot be brothers without a father. Nor can there be a brotherhood of man apart from a recognition of the Fatherhood of God. The Covenant of the League of Nations did not even mention God, so it is no wonder that the League has not been more successful than it has. "Glory to God in the highest" and then, and only then, is it possible to have peace among men.

PUNCH-UPS IN SYDNEY'S DOMAIN

The Communist Party was a bit on the nose at the moment in Australian politics. Its trouble stemmed from the fact that four months earlier, Russia had entered into a series of pacts with Germany, who was not seen to be a good bed-fellow. On top of that, Russia was now preparing to batter the Finns to death. So, the Reds here were divided amongst themselves, and decidedly on the back foot.

However, this did not keep the more militant of them from doing their normal Sunday oratory at the Domain. This wonderful parkland was host every Sunday to political parties of all sorts who had some axe to grind, or some policy to preach. At times, the dozens of speakers, some of them standing on soap-boxes, would collectively drawn a crowd of 10,000 listeners. In early 1940, with war imminent, the crowds were very large, and increasing weekly.

So the Communists turned out each week and preached the glories of Russia, and the need for Australia to seek different forms of Government. For the last month, patriotic soldiers from the Second AIF had turned out as well, with the specific purpose of heckling the Reds, and disrupting their platform. Most weeks, a little bit of pushing and shoving happened, and the police were called in to separate the revelers. The following Letter gives us a glimpse of this.

Letters, T Hunter. As one who was close enough to the speakers in the Domain last Sunday to hear clearly what was being said, I can witness that of several speakers to whom I listened, not one made a remark to which even the thinned-skinned patriot could take exception. On the contrary, speaker after speaker emphasised that they had no quarrel with the soldiers and wished them well. Notwithstanding these sentiments, an almost continuous barrage of tomatoes was aimed at the speakers. Any impartial witness, one would think, would have had little difficulty in deciding on which side restraint was exercised.

To a lover of democracy and freedom, the most disturbing feature of the proceedings was not so much the conduct of the soldiers as the demeanour of a large section of the onlookers who were only interested in the satisfaction of watching a number of men being pelted with tomatoes. For a people calling themselves a democracy, it was a disgraceful exhibition, the very antithesis of democratic and sportsman-like conduct. One is forced to conclude that our much-vaunted love of democracy and freedom is not nearly so deeply rooted as we had supposed, since in a large section of the community the totalitarian mentality lies perilously close to the surface.

REFUGEES FOR AUSTRALIA?

Hitler's persecution of the Jews was continuing, and a fortunate few were able to exit their homeland. Australia was interested in providing a haven for them, but they had to fit into our quota, along with other persons. Professor Steinberg proposed setting up settlements for Jews in Australia's Kimberley region in uninhabited North-West Australia.

Letters, G Buchanan. I wish to comment, if I may, on Dr I Steinberg's proposal to settle refugee

Jews on part of that country. Nature there has not been niggardly in providing fertile fields for governments, or others, with vision enough to apply the dynamics of science, industry, and finance to that remote but potentially prolific land. But, if we value our latent self-sufficiency and self-respect, **that country must be developed by the people whose job it is - Australians.**

Our reluctance in the last 40 years to face and enter those spheres of development where self-dependence and duty to our heritage can be achieved is evidenced by the apparent **readiness among all shades of political thought to give a measure of support to Dr Steinberg's offer**. They say, inferentially, let some foreigner reap the harvest from our difficult but accessible assets. Let some outsider do it, while we in the big cities play "two-up", throw cocktail parties, and squander our income on scenic roads, street alignments, and other civic conveniences and luxuries!

The internal policy of Australia is conceived on wrong lines, on Old World ideas quite unadaptable to a new continent learning a new, yet fundamental, economic culture. Australia is crying from our slums to have its wealth distributed, first of all, to its own people. Before we can raise, by sane development, a population which will make Australia unassailable, there are several devils to cast out – and the greatest is orthodox finance. Finance can be based only on the proved ability of our brawn, brain, and courage to extract economic and national security from our great national **resources.**

Letters, M Duff. It is apparent that we only become zealous about Australia's potential when outsiders are prepared to develop what we have neglected. We Australians depend too much on Government, and not enough on our own brawn and initiatives, and the lure of the city's pleasure deters us from putting our shoulders to the wheel.

Jewish young men are far less likely to drift back to the cities than Australians, from the fact that throughout their history they have been up against hard conditions. Given opportunity, they are prepared to work and to stick at it, and make a success of their enterprise, as they have demonstrated in Palestine.

ACTION, PLEASE, ON DIVORCE

Letters, "Yet Another Victim". I have been waiting for ten years for insanity to be made a ground for divorce. Surely, when every other State in the Commonwealth has brought in this measure, the mother State should not allow such a grave injustice to continue. Even conservative Britain has made insanity over a period of three years grounds for divorce.

My partner has been in a mental hospital for ten years, and merely because I am domiciled in New South Wales, I have to suffer this intolerable injustice. Surely uniformity of divorce laws throughout the Commonwealth is reasonable and just. How long must I wait?

FEBRUARY: OZ TROOPS ARRIVE IN EGYPT

For Britain, February was much the same as last month. Her Air Force was still fighting desultory air battles against the Hun over Scottish waters and the North Sea, and she was apparently breaking about even. A new venture was to fly further and further into Germany, not with the intention of bombing cities or even strategic targets like railways and mines, but rather to drop pamphlets urging the gullible citizens below to pull out of their unjust war.

The Airmen were so delicate in this that they were instructed to throw out the material, not in bundles that would burst open on landing, but to open the bundles in the planes and then release them. The idea was to not cause any damage when the bundles as such fell on property, or someone's head. All sides were keen to not bomb the others' cities, because of the fear of retaliation.

The Navy experienced some of its worst weeks of the War so far, in terms of **merchant navy** losses. Still, Germany was also having a hard time, and its production of submarines was scarcely able to keep up with demolition of its fleet. But torpedoes and mines were taking a severe toll on the shipping of Britain and the neutral countries.

The Army was ensconced mainly in the Maginot Line, and thereabouts. When they needed to go out to do patrols, or make occasional forays, they encountered little resistance provided they kept close to home. But it was cold, they were away from their loved ones, and they never knew when the War would hot up, and then they might be killed.

THE FIGHT IN FINLAND

Matters there were taking a sinister turn. Slowly, the Russians were adjusting to the Finns way of making war, and by the middle of the month, had started to take back some of the territory they had forsaken. By the end of the month, they had penetrated into parts of the Mannerheim Line, the huge defensive Line of armaments that the Finns were relying on.

At about this time, the top politicians of Finland flew to Britain to formally ask Britain for troops and materials so they could continue to fight. The Brits were genuinely sympathetic, but were reluctant to take on Russia. So they said they would think about it.

They did do something. Up till now, existing laws forbade recruiting of citizens for the purpose of fighting someone else's war against a friendly State. Russia was regarded as a friendly State. So, any talk of forming a volunteer Finnish army was pointless. The Letter below hoped to change that.

Letters, Constance Malleson, Blagdon, Somerset. Finland cannot stand alone – for ever. The letter from Lord Plymouth pleads for the 500,000 people homeless in Finland: the 175,000 women; the 250,000 children; the 75,000 men. We have seen in The Times pictures of Rovaniemi – bombed. We have read of Vlipuri – destroyed. We have witnessed, day after day, the profane spectacle of a nation (the most innocent and respected in Europe) assaulted, martyred, tortured almost unto death. We have borne all this and have yet kept our sanity. Why? Because we have been straining every nerve for one thing only – to help Finland.

All that we English can give, even to our lives, cannot ever repay one tittle of the debt we owe her. Every speech made by Finnish statesmen and prelates, every word reported as spoken by Finnish soldiers and civilians, has been compact of humanity. There has been no joy in "liquidating" thousands of the enemy, only a sense of the pity of wholesale slaughter – whether of poor and ignorant Russians or of democratic Finns.

If some few Englishmen can fight for Finland, and – what is more important – fight in that spirit, they will not lack a place in the hierarchy of upright men of all nations.

Comment. Pressure mounted. Before the end of February, this law was removed from the statute books, so such a volunteer army became a possibility. Granted it would take months to get off the ground, but it was a symbolic move that might have real effects if the Finnish War lasted that long. Mind you, at this stage, it was a big "if".

WHAT WERE PEOPLE AT HOME DOING?

Clearly, they doing the only thing one can do if your men–folk go away to fight a war. **They were knitting.** Woollen socks, scarves, balaclavas, ear muffs, you name it. Anything to keep freezing soldiers warm in the Northern European winter. A Feature writer from the London *Times* has a bit to say on the subject.

> Domestic experience confirms the suspicion that no matter what the difficulties or expense, wool is procured, needles are found, and knitting is openly practiced. At the end of his homeward way the weary breadwinner may be just about to sink into one of his own drawing-room chairs when he catches sight of some dreadful creature. It could be a porcupine or hedgehog, but not

with bristles pointing naturally in one direction but instead most unnaturally in all directions. And there it lies in wait for him. Swiftly but cautiously he seeks another chair. Another beast is there.

He would try again, but by this time he has somehow got his feet entangled in coils of wool, thick dark blue wool and thinner khaki wool, which unwinds itself with malignant speed from balls that were hiding under the chairs. Unless he is wise enough to keep still and shout for help, he will begin to feel like Gulliver bound in Lilliput before he is rescued and reproached.

This state of bliss was marred somewhat by the persistent shortage of wool. As you might expect, the Government had some words of solace and wisdom. These were issued as follows in a News Letter distributed by the **Depot for Knitted Garments for the Royal Navy**.

All wool is now under a Controller, to whom application has to be made for release, and this often takes several weeks. ….

It is some indication of the widespread demand which has sprung up for knitting wool that this organization alone has some 1,600 sub-depots, each of which has a minimum membership of 12 knitters, knitting wool bought through the Personal Service League obtained at a special cheap rate. The method is available only to certain recognized bodies, chief among which are Comfort Funds of the Lords Lieutenant, those of the Royal Navy and Royal Air Force, and over 60 regimental Comfort Funds for the Army, the Red Cross and St. John Ambulance

Brigade, Women's Voluntary Services, and the Women's Institutes.

If other organizations of reasonable size make application the League does its best to meet their wants, but it cannot deliver wool to individuals or small groups; their channel of supply is the retail trade. There would therefore seem to be obvious advantages in being affiliated to one of the larger organizations in touch with the Personal Service League.

When criticisms are directed against the sale of wool by the British Government to the United States, it should be remembered that the export trade of this country has to be maintained as a means of paying for imports of vital war supplies. The Joint Rationing Committee of the Wool Control believes an early increase of wool exports to be so necessary that it has lately, at the request of manufacturers and merchants, announced its decision to stimulate exports by allocating additional wool for this purpose at the expense of home trade.

Comment. Somehow, though, knitting went on, and indeed Australian knitters also made big contributions.

MEAT RATIONING IN BRITAIN

Meat was added to the list of commodities that were now to be rationed. The Times made the following comments.

Another step along the road to rationing was announced yesterday. As from March 11, the weekly ration of butcher's meat will be whatever 1s. 10d. will buy for people over six, and half that amount for children under six. It has been no secret that some such scheme was in the offing; and it does indeed complete the system of the control of meat which has already proceeded as far as making the Ministry of Food the purchaser and fixing the prices at which different cuts and qualities may be sold.

The scheme, as now published, follows the lines of rationing during the last War, except that coupons will not have to be surrendered for meals in restaurants and canteens; and the reason for fixing the ration by value instead of by weight is that the customer will be able to have a choice between different qualities of meat. This feature of the scheme will enable slender purses to go farther. The figure of value has been fixed in relation to the volume of anticipated supplies, and, though it may seem small, the housewife will probably find that it will buy not less than the usual consumption of the household, particularly if account be taken of the numerous forms of meat which will still be unrationed.

It is however true that the total amount of meat consumed will have to be less, because the amount of imported meat required for the Forces means that home-produced meat will form a larger proportion of the whole. The proper deduction is that this rationing scheme constitutes a new argument against waste, both by the Forces and by civilians, and a new reason for the fullest possible utilization of supplies.

Comment. Ration books, with their coupons, were issued to each person, and everyone suspected that, despite the fairly generous quota allowed initially, worse was likely in the future. But all these coupons that were being created out of nothing had one good result for the economy. **Black markets in coupons and commodities** came into being, and thrived right throughout the War.

But things were now to get really bad.

Press report. In a written Parliamentary reply to Dr Little, Mr Morrison, Minister of Food, states that, in view of the limited supply of cereals available for animal-feeding stuffs, the Government are making an Order restricting the output of **whisky** and other potable spirits, for the current year **to one-third of last year's production**. The output of beer will be permitted to continue at a level not exceeding that of last year.

To minimize inconvenience to the industries concerned, Advisory Committees representative of distillers, brewers, and maltsters are being set up by the Ministry of Food. Steps will be taken to ensure that purchases of cereals for brewing or distilling are not made in excess of requirements for this year's permitted production.

The consumption of sugar for brewing will, in accordance with arrangements made for the reduction of supplies for other industrial purposes, be reduced to 70 per cent of normal requirements. Supplies of cereals will, if necessary, be available to meet the deficiency. Mr Morrison adds that he has been assured of the cooperation of industries concerned.

BRITISH HOME PROPAGANDA

The Brits were always determined that the free flow of information and freedom of speech were the cornerstones of democracy and liberty. So, of course, they were anxious that the various kinds of propaganda organizations now set up were forced to keep their proper place. Right now, the unnecessary censorship of non-essential news, and blatant lies were getting up their noses.

For example, a report, in the Times, said that Russian bombers over Finland had dropped 3,000 bombs in one day, with only one death resulting. This was regarded widely as a lie. Another report said that the British flagship, the Nelson, had been damaged and withdrawn temporarily from active service. This would not have worried anyone, except the incident happened in November, three months earlier. What use is news that is stale, people asked. Any one who wanted up-to-date news, and most folk did, could get it nightly by **tuning their short-wave radios to Berlin,** and while they might then be taking their chances with the truth, at least it was up-to-date.

The matter of propaganda and censorship remained a big problem in Britain, and also in Australia, for years to come, and we will hear more about it as we proceed.

OZ MILITARY NEWS

On February 13th, our Government pulled a rabbit out of the hat. It needed this rabbit, because it was just about to go into a by-election for a Federal seat in Corio in Victoria, and the polls showed that they were several rabbits behind. It had been losing the war-vote on a regular basis. Many people thought that its policies were all over the place, and hardly hung together. For example, the critics of its chopping and changing in its recruitment of soldiers were legion. So too were its critics of the meagre pay the servicemen were receiving, and the half-hearted way in which they had been outfitted.

Others were complaining about the fact we were not really gearing up for an all-out war, but were simply nibbling at the edges. Voters clearly were alienated one way or another, and if only Curtin would drop his resistance to our servicemen serving overseas, the Labour Party would be set to win in Corio and probably lots of other places in due course.

So, in a remarkable coincidence of timing, out popped the rabbit. The trouble was that it was a dead rabbit. It was supposed to be a surprise, to bring transports of joy, to make us gasp with delight, and say "aren't they clever". But rabbits that have been dead for a month rarely do that.

What they announced on the 13th was that the Sixth Division of the Second AIF had landed in the Middle East, and let it be leaked that they were probably in Egypt. "Surprise, Surprise", you might exclaim. But you would be wrong. Only last month the troops of the AIF marched through Sydney's streets in a grand parade. Well, after that they got on ships and set off toward the enemy. Half of Sydney was there to send them off. As they went westwards to Perth, a few more million people saw them at wharfs as the ships stopped for victuals. But this was supposed to be a hush-hush affair. **The newspapers were not allowed to publish one word about this transportation** because of the specious excuse that no one wanted the enemy to find out about it. So, it was kept under wraps until just before Corio. This was a very dead rabbit.

It was also a public relations disaster for other reasons. Several hours after Menzies released the information on the landing in Egypt, he found out that the Admiralty in London, in advance of Australia, had already made the announcement, and further, that they had issued more news than the restricted summary he had been permitted to broadcast here.

Menzies was furious at this latter event, and he used the word "stupid" several times in describing the people involved. In the long run, he realised that having a civil Department of Information, as well as an Army Censorship Bureau, was never going to work, and put officials to work to sort it out, and get a bit of sense into the system. He also delivered some messages, doubtless full of good cheer, to London on the matter.

OUR AIR FORCE

The Government did better in a series of announcements about the Air Force. It was well known that it planned that a large numbers of young men would be trained, and sent to Britain. At last, something more definite was announced, and seemed likely to happen.

The gist of the announcements was that some 50 thousand males would be trained under the Empire Air Scheme. Initially, they would get instruction from local aero clubs, but that would quickly give way to more formal Air Force training as barracks, trainer planes, uniforms and equipment became available. Within a few months, thousands of them would be sent overseas, and it was expected that this would be a great relief to the besieged airmen already fighting in Britain. The regular Air Force would also continue to recruit, though how these two ventures would interleave was not clear as yet.

OZ NEWS AND VIEWS IN OZ

Letters, J Macarthur Onslow. This morning an officer from the University Regiment, which is in camp for training some two miles from my home, came to me with the following message from his C.O. That the medical officer of the camp forbids the use of the water from the Nepean River, which is close by the camp, as being insanitary. Could I, therefore, allow my private water supply for the use of the troops?

I quite agree that the river water is insanitary and unhygienic, as its flow is stopped for the use of the Sydney water supply. But the Australian troops are called up by the government, and are sent for training to camp on the local racecourse. The Sydney water supply canal runs close by the camp. But NSW law forbids them to use or to take water from the canal.

If I allow my tank to be used by the troops, in a few days my household must be drinking the Nepean River puddle water, or migrate. This I should do willingly, but my tank water will not last the troops more than a few days.

Fortunately, the houses on the Camden Park property are on the Sydney water supply, and I have told the Officer Commanding to draw what water he needs and can find there from the taps in those houses. But what we should have made very plain to us is which law prevails, and whether the New South Wales Government and law is competent to destroy Australian troops by thirst – or force them to rely on the goodwill and charity of private citizens for the first necessity of life.

In France the commanding officer would take the water if necessary by an armed guard. In England he would telephone to district command or to the War Office. In Germany he'd simply shoot whoever tried to prevent him. But here he is forced to beg.

FOR OWNERS OF DRAFT HORSES

Those breeders **who maintained their faith in the draught horse would yet reap their reward** for their persistency in breeding and improving the Clydesdale studs of the Commonwealth, despite discouraging conditions.

"Once having embarked on the formation of a Clydesdale stud, it is foolish to throw in the towel at the first sign of a drop in the market," declared Mr Comans, President of the NSW Branch of the Clydesdale Horse Society, in an appeal to stud-owners to keep up their adult registrations in accordance with the society's rules.

It was a short-sighted policy, he said, that immediately a slackness took place in the horse trade, breeders should neglect registering. The present phase in the horse industry was not going to last indefinitely; consequently, the breeder should be in a position to meet the improved market when it came.

During the period from 1922 to 1930, when horse trading conditions were difficult, there had been a tendency to neglect the adult registration of animals, said Mr Comans. Many disposed of their studs and ceased breeding. When a change for the better in the market asserted itself in

1930, these people started to buy and continued to do so on a rising market for four or five years. Then, as soon as there was a drop in values, they immediately started to sell, or ceased to carry on with their registrations in the stud book.

Actually, a period of inactive trading should be welcomed by Clydesdale breeders, as it offered an excellent opportunity to cull the surplus and inferior animals, leaving only the best mares from which to breed. In that way, the standard of Clydesdales could be materially improved, particularly as there was not the inducement to keep too many colts entire.

At the same time it was desirable that breeders should maintain their studs at a reasonable level. By breeding from the best mares, and by using a sire that would improve the standard of the stud, definite headway could be achieved.

NOW, LISTEN HERE

In 1940, the humble telephone was not quite so humble, and less than half the houses in this fair land had one installed. In the outer suburbs of the major cities, and in all country towns, there was a scarcity of these contrivances, and this was sometimes alleviated by installing a single line to perhaps six homes, and they shared the joys of listening to each other's conversations. Apart from this inconvenience, there were other problems, for example the billing system.

Letters, J Bousfield. The whole point in having party lines is to reduce the cost by getting rentals from a number of people instead of one, and it is quite unreasonable to reverse the process after three people are admitted to a line and make subscribers pay more individually instead of less. This, I maintain, is an unreasonable and absurd state of affairs brought about by a fault in the regulations which provide a reduction per capita for persons up to three on a line, and then turns round and reverses the process by charging more per head for the unlucky fourth or fifth.

Comment. This Letter is just a reminder that party lines were a menace. Probably the biggest nuisance was the teen-age girl who would get on and keep talking for hours. This reduced or stalled others from using it for their purposes. Still, what else do you do when you do not have enough equipment?

LETTER FROM A MOTHER

Letters, Mary Tonner. I am as patriotic as any one else. But it is too much that some matrons in this town are now looking down their noses at young men who have not joined the services, and saying behind their backs that they are too scared to fight. Some are even branded as cowards. Why my sons are not in the Services is no one else's business, and whether they join up in the future is also no one else's business.

MARCH: FINLAND FALLS

On March 3rd, the Russian military opened offensives all over Finland and, by the 13th, that country had fully capitulated. All those weeks spent kidding themselves that they could withstand the Russian Bear had come to nought, and they were forced to accept far harsher and more debilitating terms than any that had been proposed earlier. **The war in Finland was over.** In two week's time she would sign peace treaties that would guarantee her independence, but actually grant her none. By June, she would be fully integrated into the Soviet State, and remain there until the fall of the Red bloc fifty years later.

With the action over, all the recrimination started. France and Britain now fell over themselves in pointing out what good fellows they had been. France said that she had 50,000 troops ready to go to Finland's aid on March 5th, but that she could not send them because Norway and Sweden would not grant them permission to cross their nations to get to Finland. The French Premier, Daladier (our version of the Prime Minister), pointed out that the League of Nations demanded that foreign troops could not cross another country without permission. So, he said, beating his breast, I could not send my 50,000. What a bugger.

Britain's Chamberlain waited until the day before Finland capitulated to say that Britain was prepared to "proceed immediately to Finland's help, using all the available resources at our disposal." This sounded like a horde of troops, and this would have meant fighting the Russians. A Labour Member asked "Is this tantamount to going to war with Russia?" To which Chamberlain replied "We have not arrived at that yet." When asked if his statement meant that he was proposing to actually send troops, he replied "I cannot add to my statement." In other words "not on your life."

In fact, both of these fine gentlemen had known that peace talks had been going on since February 25th, and that fighting was about to finish. So now they became vocal, offering whatever they thought was enough to cover themselves, knowing full well that they would never be called on to deliver.

Public outcry over these deceptions and over the fate of Finland was extensive and voluble. The two other Scandinavian nations, Norway and Sweden, were not at all keen to be painted as villains, and this comes out in the following letter from the Consul-General in Sydney.

Letters, Carlo De Dardel, Consul-General of Sweden, Sydney. Thousands of Swedes of military age are fighting side by side with the Finns, commanded by Swedish officers and fully equipped from Swedish sources. Apart from this, Sweden has sent military supplies to the limit of her capacity; Finnish wounded are received into Swedish hospitals; ten thousand homes in Sweden have opened their doors to Finnish refugees, and millions of pounds have been subscribed for whatever purpose the Finnish Government may choose.

Factory workers have set aside their overtime pay for the Finns, and retail shops have given the earnings of one day to the same cause; already in January subscriptions amounted to about one Australian pound from every man, woman, and child in Sweden, and they continue still to pour in. Hospitals, ambulances, and Swedish doctors in considerable numbers are on the Finnish front, and appeals for volunteers and funds are broadcast over the official Swedish radio.

Regarding the present peace negotiations, the Swedish Government has put no pressure on Finland, according to the official Swedish wireless. The Swedish Government has acted only as an intermediary between an almost inexhaustible Russia and a Finland which must shortly be devastated, lacking the necessary support to continue the war. It is impossible to deny that, with all Britain's goodwill, the material support has until now been inadequate, and what has gone, as must be obvious to anyone familiar with geography has necessarily been transported through Swedish territory. Indeed, it would be more than extraordinary if Sweden, with all the help she has given Finland, should have prevented the transit of this material, thus conniving at the death, not only of thousands of Finns, but of her own sons.

The transit of a foreign army is naturally in another category; it would constitute a definite breach of neutrality, and would probably provoke a German attack on Sweden, which would necessitate the immediate cessation of assistance to Finland and the concentration of all Sweden's might in the south. However, the question of an allied army crossing Sweden cannot become concrete unless and until the Allies declare war on Russia, a course which seems far from their present policy.

There was other criticism. It was argued that the League of Nations had virtually gone out of existence. No one paid any attention to it at all. How could the Allies then resurrect the League's rules only selectively to sanctify their own positions?

Letters, E Holme. I have just heard from the Town Hall a magnificent rendering of "Finlandia." That music now embodies for me the soul of a just and valiant people, which ought to be the pride of whatever is left worth living in Europe. It forms, for me, an International Anthem in the one universal language, that of musical sound. If it could be adopted as such and if the example just given us by the Finns could be followed throughout the nations that preserve some relics of faith, truth, and honesty, they should be able to overcome the Blatant Beast of our time, companion of Envy and Detraction.

The model of freedom and self-government, consistent even to the point of self-immolation for principle, which Finland has given us in the only chance fate allowed it, that of liberty for the last twenty years, might then suffice for the necessary reconstruction of the political systems of Europe. Finland has offered us the moral inspiration needed for the ending of seventy years of German terror, and regeneration of the European peoples, including those of Germany.

Comment. It is easy to be critical of the two Heads of Government in sending aid that was merely token. But, on the other hand, here were two countries, Russia and Finland, coming to blows, and **Britain was officially friends with both of them**. When it was clear from the beginning that one of them would win easily, would it have been sense to send troops for one of them, and almost certainly end up fighting with the other? Did Britain want to go to war with Russia? Did she think Finland important enough to send her own sons off to be killed for her fight for freedom? Could she sustain a war with Russia at the same time as she was struggling with Germany? Should Finland in the first place have anticipated the inevitable, and accepted Russian domination, and **saved the lives of a hundred thousand Finnish men?**

I can understand why Chamberlain refused to get involved. I could wish he had devised a better way to do things, but even now, with all the extra information that has since been revealed, I have no idea of what he could have done better.

The growth of impatience. With the collapse of Finland, there was a noticeable change in the British (and French) attitude to the War. There had been previously a thankfulness that the War had degenerated into a Phoney War, with little actual land combat. This seemed so much better than the trench warfare of WW1. Now, it seemed that resolve was stiffening up. The nation had seen what happened to Finland, when Britain had delayed and procrastinated, for whatever reason. But people were getting fed-up with this approach, and the mood was switching to "**Let's get on with it**." Even here, in Oz, the *Sydney Morning Herald* of March 27th, had that exact phrase as leader on its Editorial. In Britain, public pressure for more positive action was on the rise, and politicians would surely be forced to heed it.

OZ MILITARY NEWS

Comment. In one of my rare moments of tolerance towards mankind, I confess that I feel a bit sorry for the Oz Government and the armed forces. Here in 1940, they were rightly copping criticism from all over the place about their preparations for war, and how nothing fitted together. But I must say in their defence that too much was happening, and all of it was happening at once. A year ago, the then Prime Minister, Joseph Lyons, was hoping he could get by with recruiting 70,000 men for a part-time militia with only three months of training. Yet here we had Bob Menzies now confronted with a large contingent of AIF in Egypt, and airmen about to join them by the thousands, and a hundred thousand more men about to be recruited, and probably sent overseas as well.

In that year, troops had to be recruited, housed, armed and equipped, fed, wet-nursed, paid, trained, and what-have-you. The troops needed to find out about tanks, searchlights, ack-ack guns, horses, tank traps, hand grenades, a wide range of guns and artillery, balloons and more what-have-you. To put all this together in the right order, in the right amounts, with the right people was an impossible task. So if they were doing it by the well-established method of error-and-trial-and-error, I can excuse them a bit.

Still, that does not stop me from reporting some criticism of military activities.

Letters, Militiaman, Rutherford Camp. The many militia cooks now in various military camps in New South Wales work on an average 18 hours per day for seven days every week, and when they went for their cooking test were definitely promised the small pay of 10/- per day. On this understanding they gave up their employment, left their comfortable homes, wives, and families, and went into camp at Rutherford. After toiling for many days in broiling kitchens they were refused their modest promise of 10/- per day, and only given a paltry wage of 8/- per day. In spite of protests, no redress has been obtained, and an appeal is made for justice in this matter.

Compare the starvation rates of pay for these highly skilled and certificated militia cooks with the rates paid to civilian cooks in military camps. These civilian cooks receive 16/8 per day with double time for every Sunday and all holidays. They are paid an average of 6 Pounds 15 shillings per week as against 2 Pounds 16 shillings for militia cooks. Many of these civilian cooks are young single men of eligible military age, yet they receive more than double the pay of the unfortunate patriotic militia cook, who is even refused his pathetic promised 10/- per day. An appeal is made to those responsible to remedy this injustice.

Letters, M Byrnes. Whilst no sane person would question the need for reasonable censorship in time of war, surely some better plan can be evolved than to cut our soldiers' letters into pieces. Last week I received, by air mail, a letter from my son on active service overseas, and whole sentences were cut out, as well as place names, evidently names which had been published in every paper and broadcast from every radio station in the Commonwealth a week before.

For economy, both sides of paper are used, so that much on the reverse is destroyed by cutting. Three of my sons served in the last war, and on no occasion was a letter cut, though a word or clause was sometimes obliterated. A rubber stamp would surely save much of the censor's valuable time.

JINGOISM IS GROWING

With armed troops serving overseas, and massive preparations for war being made, it was hardly surprising that patriotism was on the increase. Most people took a moderate view, and while they were aware of the dangers surrounding this nation, they were prepared to wait a while, and cool down a bit **After all, it was Britain under attack, not Australia.**

A few however were indeed getting worked up and put themselves into print with all their fervour.

Letters, R Downer. The Governor's speech at the opening of the Royal Show was indeed inspiring. A "united national effort" is a worthwhile battle-cry. But complementary to this clarion call came a well-timed warning from the Premier. Is this a time for "complacency"? Because of our unique and happy position, so apparently secure and immune from attack, with life so generally prosperous and easy-going, it is only too easy to relapse into complacency.

Let us turn to the other side of the picture and see Europe locked in a death grapple. Ruined, devastated, and pillaged countries, beaten to a pulp by merciless bullies; our own Mother country so bravely enduring severe business dislocation, an enormous income tax burden, rationing, darkness, and, above all, the anxiety of having fathers, sons, husbands, brothers at the front, in the air, and on the sea.

Must we not steel ourselves to sacrifice, too? In our great democracy for which we are fighting service is a freewill offering. Grumblers and slackers are traitors to the cause. Is it a time to carp at prices received, to strike, to preach self, to show apathy, or offer little but criticism? I lived in Germany during the Boer War. There, forty years ago, "Der Tag" was gloated over; perhaps good naturedly by my young German acquaintances; but, notwithstanding, the threat was there. Mealy-mouthedness is not for such a time as this, and decades of hate lie at Germany's door.

Australia has never failed, and will never fail. But our torches must be kept alight, or the darkness will fall – here, in this beautiful and blessed land.

OZ NEWS AND TRIVIA

Rev Gibb of Moree started a controversy by saying that prayers to God for rain were pointless, and indeed they were insulting to God by asking for intervention in trivial matters that were clearly were intended to be part of life's struggles.

Letters, S.M. Rev Gibb refers to prayers for rain, as an "Ignorant Travesty" and dangerous to true religion. As a layman holding office in one of the city churches, I think these utterances most indiscreet, and repugnant to our God-fearing people of the community.

It surpasses understanding how any cleric of any denomination, could allow himself to drift so far from the doctrines of the church in which he was ordained. Mr Gibb says that prayers do not affect the weather, but can he explain why in past occasions, when the country has been in the grip of the drought, and prayers have been offered up for rain in the various churches, in a very short period, those rains have come and replenished the earth. Even as now, only a few hours after services concluded last Sunday, heavy showers were with us, and inland quite good falls have taken place.

Finally, would Mr Gibb inform us, why in the Great War, when England was losing badly, the late King and his Parliament called the whole of the British Nation to prayer (National Prayer), and from that day, victory was won?

Letters, Edward Masey. The fact that rain fell on the day following the prayers proves little, apart from the fact that the Churches chose their moment well. The weather prophets have been promising rain for some weeks past; and the efficacy of prayers might be better tested if they were offered at the beginning, rather than the end, of a drought, at a time when the experts were predicting no possible prospects of rain.

But what does God do when some people pray for rain and others pray that it will not rain? Certain crops need dry weather at harvest, because the crop will rot if it gets wet. If God sends rain at the wrong time, everything will be lost. Do you think that maybe he can send rain on a farm-by-farm basis? Perhaps, if we ask him nicely, he will do it on a paddock-by-paddock basis. Perhaps, he might go so far as to just fill up the bucket near the chook shed? Or perhaps he has a bit of sense, and says the weather is the weather, and you have to take your chance.

Letters, W Hartley. Your correspondent, M Hill, declares that the Great War proves the value of prayer. Instead, it is a striking illustration of its ineffectiveness, for surely in the history of the world no greater volume of prayer, from the mothers of all nations, has ever ascended to heaven. Yet not only was there no evidence of divine interposition, but the cause of that conflict is still as active as ever. Man makes war and he must end it; there is no other way.

Letters, Luma Retna. Rev Gibb has put his finger on the major reason why the various Churches are continually complaining of a lack of religious adherents. True knowledge has brought the present generation to a point where many cannot accept the churches' teachings or interpretation of natural phenomena. Whilst I firmly believe that eventually science and religion will walk hand in hand, there is much on which the Churches should alter their interpretation. Science has taken away our past beliefs in regard to thunder and lightning, and brought those beliefs from a supernatural standpoint to one where we see the occurrence as a perfectly natural phenomenon. In time we will do the same with such attempts as rainmaking through prayer which can be relegated to a past superstitious age. They can only retard the true progress of the Church, which, if it only could deliver its message properly, could do much more than it is at present to save a civilisation from attempting to destroy itself.

GIRLS ARE SMOKING

Smoking by girls and youths was strongly criticised by speakers who addressed the Methodist Conference at the Lyceum yesterday. The Rev Lock said that continual smoking was helping to build a race weak in body and feeble in mind. Some children were cursed from birth because their mothers were addicted to smoking.

Dr W McClelland said that smoking was harmful to young people, especially to the delicate nervous mechanism of women and girls. The Rev H Doust said that he did not believe that smoking was wicked, but he did not like it. "I think that we shall lay ourselves open to a charge of hypocrisy if we ask young people not to smoke while we ourselves continue to make a habit of it," he said. "The implication in this debate," said Mr T Taylor "is that **a man who smokes is not a Christian**. If we are to be consistent, we ought to have an anti-cosmetics league and an anti-everything league."

Another resolution commended the Federal Government for its policy of dry canteens in camps, and urged an extension of the system to all ranks, officers and sergeants. The Government was also urged to consider the advisability of prohibiting the custom of **shouting for drinks during the period of the war** and demobilisation.

It was also decided to ask the State Government to refuse to issue any more licences for mechanical hare coursing.

A BRIT SPEAKS OUT

Letters, Disillusioned Pommy. It is a odd and baffling mystery how Australians, collectively so loyal to the Empire as shown by their magnificent war effort, **can be individually so unfriendly to Britishers in their midst**. No good purpose can be served by ignoring the fact – all too evident in many ways – that Australians, on the whole, have some lingering doubts in their minds about our bona fides, our honesty, our worth, our sincerity, call it what you will. It is hard to explain, and yet we meet at every turn this suspicion, this proneness to harsh criticism and unfair judgment, and many of us wonder what national characteristic we possess which excited so much distrust or ill-feeling.

The average Australian man will not budge an inch to assist a Britisher floundering in the quagmire of economic difficulties. Should you come from Vienna, Prague, or Warsaw, the Australian will be immensely interested in you, and take no end of trouble to find you a niche in industry or the professions. You will find him the good Samaritan par excellence. But should you hail from Belfast, Birmingham, or Glasgow, you are cold-shouldered and left to your own resources to sink or swim. To the working class Australian, especially, your presence is an intrusion and your accent a joke. He's not going to give you an opening in industry if he can help it, and he won't let you into his union.

Australia is the only country in the world where you will find people of British stock sunk so low in the social scale as to work in a servile capacity for foreigners. In Sydney thousands of young men and women depend for their livelihood on people who could not read a leading article in the "Herald", much less speak the language properly. So much for our imperial race!

When the spirit of nationality, which is the life-blood of a country, no longer runs pure from the parent source, when other streams trickle in from other directions, you will never build up a great nation inspired by pride of race, common ideals and unity of purpose. Then "Advance, Australia Fair" will have no meaning and no hope for the future. Out of the melting pot that is Australia today, there will emerge no great and free people unless you maintain the predominance of your British stock, and have periodical renewal – of that stock **from the heart of the mother country itself**.

FISH FOR WAR EFFORT.

Letters, Bob Clifford. The Tuggerah Lakes Fishermen's Association has decided that each man will give two boxes of fish for local war funds, and we as a body of men are appealing to all fishermen in New South Wales to help us build up the war fund and do our part for our fellow-fishermen and others who have joined the colours. We also ask fishermen of other States to join and help the good cause. Each man must put his shoulder to the wheel for freedom's sake and help in every way he can, for the test is now on, and we fishermen love freedom.

APRIL: ACTION IN NORWAY

Given that there was a war going on, the first three months of 1941 had been relatively quiet. Sadly, this situation was about to change, and all hell was about to break loose. In April, attention had switched back to Germany, and the hapless victims were Norway and Holland. At the same time, as we will see, Britain got badly mauled.

Norway was one of three Scandinavian States that were located North of Europe proper, and separated from Europe by the Baltic Sea. Over the last few months, as we saw, a near-by State, Finland, had been invaded by Russia, and was now firmly under its control. The middle State was Sweden, and she was determined to maintain her neutrality. Norway wanted to do that too, but as it turned out, she had no say at all in the matter.

Norway was bounded on the west by the Atlantic Ocean. Hitler saw this long coastline, with four usable ports, as being valuable to him as bases for his navy. What wonderful fun he could have harassing shipping if he had free access to these. Hitler also wanted Norway because Narvak, to the far north, was capable of providing large quantities of the iron ore he needed for his war economy.

On the other hand, Britain coveted control of Norway because she wanted to stop the flow of iron ore and coal that went from there to Germany and Italy. On the third hand, Norway just wanted to trade like any neutral nation should, and to be left alone.

In recent months, she was getting cranky with the two main belligerents. **With Britain**, Norway resented **that** country violating her territorial waters. And lately, Britain had been intercepting her vessels bound for unfriendly countries, and seizing the cargoes. No wonder she was cranky. To top that off, the Brits had just started to lay mines in her territorial waters. **What utter contempt for a friendly nation and for international law!**

With Germany, Norway's ire was provoked by the sinking of a few of her merchant vessels by submarines, which were prone to shoot first and not stay round to ask questions. She was not game to say too much to the German bully because of the ever-present fear of that nation.

All of these tensions came to a head on April 8th. That morning, a German fleet, with thousands of soldiers, set sail for the four ports in Norway. On the same day, a British fleet of comparable size also set out for the same ports. While they were sailing north, Hitler decided to fill the waiting time by occupying Denmark, also on the northern limits of Europe proper, and in four hours was able to gain her consent to his taking over the running of the economy. This invasion was almost bloodless, with only 20 men killed in the process. Here, of course, the lessons from Finland had been learned. What was the point of holding out hopelessly? As it turned out, Hitler adopted a benevolent attitude to the compliant Danes, and while they lost control, and freedom of speech, his occupation was relatively painless.

In the meantime, Hitler's troops and fleets got to Norway **first**, on April 9th. They quickly suppressed most opposition, and any that remained took up positions in the mountains that surrounded the handful of ports being occupied. The first sign that the British were not happy with this occupation was seen two days later when a British flotilla breezed into the harbour at Narvik, and destroyed one third of the German vessels there. Then, in case there was still any misunderstanding of her displeasure, two days after that the flotilla returned, and took out another one third of the boats at rest. These attacks crippled Hitler's navy for the rest of the War, and the German Navy never recovered.

On land, though, the Army was not nearly so successful. Given that the Germans had already landed and established bases at the few ports available, the British had to be selective about where they landed. They chose Narvik, in the north, and Trondheim, in Central Norway. Initially they were superior in numbers to the Germans, but the latter had control of the airfields. Using these, they were able to fly in a steady stream of fresh fighters. Also they used them as bases from which to launch an endless stream of dive-bombers that wreaked havoc. The Brits meanwhile had very little air support.

The Germans had initially landed at four major ports, and also near Oslo, the capital. The Brits had challenged at only two points, Narvik and Trondheim, so the Germans quickly over-ran the rest of the country. Their task then was to clean out the two ports where fighting continued. For the first few days, British newspapers were full of success stories. For the next week, they were more cautious, and spoke of the problems with the terrain, and difficulties of keeping up supplies. Then, they sent out signals that things were really going bad. Here in Sydney, the Editor of the *SMH* echoed these sentiments in a cautious tract that never-the-less told a depressing story.

> The statement issued last night by the Minister for External Affairs, Mr McEwen, points frankly to the difficulties which the Allies are

encountering, and is a welcome amplification of the all-too-meagre official reports which have been forthcoming from London as to the progress of the campaign. Military reticence is essential up to a point, but rumour and misleading reports from neutral sources should not be allowed to do duty for official intelligence which will enable the public to keep events in Norway in their proper perspective.

Only by an understanding of the handicaps under which the Allied forces are labouring, and which our Military Correspondent has repeatedly emphasised, is it possible to realise why progress must at best be slow, and why reverses and losses are inseparable from the attempt to dislodge a well-armed and well established foe.

Mr McEwen's statement stresses that the Allies are having to rely for the whole of their southern operations on little more than fishing ports lacking quay and harbour equipment. "When it is realised that these bases, Andaisnes and Namsos, as well as all the roads and railways serving the British forces, are being subjected to constant and intensive aerial bombardment, the difficulties confronting the Allied forces can be better appreciated. Command of the sea has permitted the Allies to land considerable bodies of troops in the teeth of obstacles which must have seemed well-nigh insuperable when it was decided that the Norwegians must be supported at all costs, but, lacking aerodromes, they have not yet been able to counter the incessant German attacks."

By the end of the month, the British forces had been withdrawn from Trondheim. By May 7th, most of them had also been taken from round Narvik, leaving a small rump to harass the Germans for another month. Over 20,000 British soldiers were shipped out to Scotland, and **the whole episode was exposed, despite all the razzamatazz, as a conspicuous failure**.

At the end of it, Norway and Denmark were in German hands, and they stayed that way till the end of the War. Germany had complete control of the access to the Baltic Sea, though it was only via her submarines that she was to have an impact at sea.

The King of Norway, Haakon VII, set up Government in Windsor, in England, and from there he directed resistance for the war years.

At the end of April, the magnitude of the ineptitude of the various levels of British leadership was just becoming apparent to the public at home. We shall see next month just how widespread this dissatisfaction became, and what various people did about it.

OZ MILITARY NEWS.

Not everyone agreed with the decision on conscientious objectors reported last month.

> **Letters, B Archibold.** At the sixth annual country convention of the UAP, a motion recommending that no exemption from military training be given to "so-called conscientious objectors" was carried without debate. One wonders what is the theological outcome of the trend of mind shown here? A significant implication is most obvious in the use of the words "so-called." Does the UAP consider there are no genuine objectors? Does this party think

conscience is dead? Of course, there are those who seek a refuge for their cowardice by playing the role of "conscientious objectors," but even "patriotism" can be the refuge of cowards. Let us credit other people with honesty, even if their views differ violently from ours.

If we are to be caught up in this "totalitarian" tendency and individuals are to be deprived of their rights as such, then we must ask, what are we fighting for? We tell ourselves we are fighting against Nazism for the preservation of democracy. What is democracy? Does it not place foremost the rights of the individual as a member of the community, and hold religious convictions sacred?

OTHER MILITARY MATTERS

Letters, AJAX. Can the postal authorities explain why letters to and from the AIF abroad are as slow in reaching their destinations or never reach them at all? My son left with the AIF in January last. Since his departure we have had three letters from him, all written at sea, but we have definite knowledge that he posted eight letters to us, all sent by airmail. What has become of the other five?

We have had no letter from him since his arrival in Palestine, though again we have definite knowledge that he has written to us every week, and has posted the letters on each occasion by airmail. I have had letters from other AIF men complaining that they have received no letters and no newspapers in cases where I know for a certainty that they have been sent and addressed correctly. Our New Postmaster-General can show of what he is made if he will cause a searching enquiry to be made into this matter.

Letters, W B T. It comes as a surprise to read in this morning's Herald that parcels for individual soldiers abroad must be examined by officials of the Lord Mayor's Fund. As the father of two lads overseas, I object to this completely unnecessary supervision, and claim the right to send comforts without parcels being picked over with the chance of the loss of some. I and my family do not object to the usual supervision and inspection of parcels by postal officials, who are men trained for the job. Surely, if the contents of a parcel is written on the package and the package left unsealed, it should be safe enough to send it.

In any case, how am I, working miles from Sydney, to get in touch with this Comforts Fund? Is there a depot in every suburb, or have I to make a trip to Sydney? Those who, like myself, have sons at the front, know well that there are many things not entirely satisfactory in the manner of dealing with our soldier boys, and while we make every allowance for war-time difficulties, we resent too much interference with our liberties.

Letters, J Bourke. Mr A Playfair of the RAS has stated that the trotting breed of horses is the most suitable for military purposes. The well-ribbed horse when crossed with a light draft produces an excellent gun horse and also sires better than the trotter. The Indian remount buyers take the progeny of blood stock first. These were the type of horse that we had in the Light Horse in the last war.

Letters, W M, Strathfield. The discarding of some types of tin containers in wartime is pure waste. Many of these tins come wrapped and lined with paper, and the container is in no way affected by its contents. Perhaps the best example is the tobacco tin. At least one tobacconist in the city is already refunding one penny for every 4oz tin returned in good condition. The price of tinplate has already increased by more than 40 per cent since the war commenced. Many traders affected by this increase should welcome an opportunity of securing sound containers.

Could not the organisers of the Lord Mayor's Patriotic and War Fund provide this opportunity, and, at the same time, augment their funds? Let them obtain from the traders interested the sole rights for resale to them of used containers. Since they already make collections of papers and rags, saved by housewives, in all suburbs, the collection of tins could be effected at very little extra cost. Lists of tins to be saved could, perhaps, be published in your columns, and Australian women would readily respond. By lessening the need for imports of tinplate, overseas exchange would be conserved and shipping space reserved for more vital imports.

COMMUNISM IN AUSTRALIA

Since 1917, Communism had gained many adherents throughout the world, and had become a powerful force.

It had gained only a small following in Australia, but because of their fiery conviction, and careful planning, they were now punching well above their weight.

In particular, they had gained many powerful positions in the Executive of Trade Unions, and while they had virtually **no power politically through elections and the ballot box,** they were in a position to frustrate capitalism through the vexing process of calling strikes willy nilly in some vital Unions. At the same time, these strikes affected the general public, and caused the ordinary householders no end of irritation.

By April, 1940, it looked like a War was really on the doorstep. The coal miners, led by Communists, were just finishing a long strike, which the Press and politicians were painting as highly devastating to the community. So, from this point of view, the Communists were on the outer. And also remember that the Russian Reds had just a few months earlier joined in non-combat treaties with the Germans, and swore they would remain friends through thick and thin. This made them very suspect in Australian eyes, and of course this rubbed off on Oz Reds.

Popular feeling against the local Reds, whipped up by the master-stirrer Robert Menzies himself, was starting to grow at a rapid rate. There were calls from all over the place for Communism to be proscribed, which meant that it would have some of its activities declared illegal, and perhaps it might be completely banned.

The Editor of the *Sydney Morning Herald* was quite keen on this idea. He called for proscription, and argued that the interests of the nation and the Empire were threatened by the Reds.

He alleged that the fact must now be faced that the subversive manifestations of Communist policy are going beyond the bounds of legitimate propaganda, and far exceeding the indulgence possible to a nation which is fighting for its existence.

The constant drip of Communist propaganda was a recognised feature of Australian politics long before the War. But with the coming of the Berlin-Moscow Pact, the instruction was issued from Moscow that "Germany is our friend and ally", and the faithful obediently gave their loyalty to the pro-Nazi Russia.

He added that the Red's crescendo of propaganda since then can only be noted with alarm, and its latest manifestation, the seditious pamphlet anonymously posted to a Cabinet Minister, may well bring matters to a head. The Postal service, maintained by the people of Australia, has been used to spread propaganda directed towards nullifying our war effort and lying accusations against Allied leaders.

So too the right of free speech, attained by desperate sacrifices in the past, was used at the Easter Conference for the purpose of asserting "Australian people have nothing to be gained from the continuance of the war," as well as pro-Russian resolutions which are an insult to the intelligence of loyal Australian men and women.

Letters, Ben Lomond. Visiting a second-hand bookstall in Sydney, I was astonished at the immense variety and quantities of Communistic books, periodicals, and newspapers on sale.

But it was still more astonishing to note the paucity of literature setting forth the democratic position; nor does this seem to have been due to the lack of desire on the bookseller's part to stock such goods.

The plain facts are, that, apart from the official publications of the British Ministry of Propaganda, and now and then a volume in the Penguin Series setting forth the viewpoint of democracy, Democracy seems singularly inept in the setting forth of its own case, and so the white-anting Communist Press Bureau has the field almost to itself. A glance at the bookshelves in a certain University library, known to the writer, serves to emphasise the truth of this.

There are scores of volumes on Russian policy and only a few dealing with the other side. If we are going to maintain our present heritage and to make it an effective weapon in the world reconstruction programme, of which the nations now dream, we must see to it that the basic principles of democracy are known and understood by all our people. Let democracy awake and put its house in order ere it is **too late.**

Letters, D Garnsey, The Rectory, West Goulburn. The prohibition of printing, distribution, and possession of Communist literature on the ground that it is enemy literature is open to several objections. First of all, it assumes that Russia is an enemy country, whereas she has declared herself neutral. Admittedly, neutrality today may be a thin veil for hostility. But Russia's neutrality cannot be shown to be primarily governed by hostility to the Allies.

Her invasion of Poland and Finland, indefensible as they were from the moral standpoint, were of very doubtful assistance to Germany. She has, moreover, certainly not helped Germany with trade and war materials any more than Italy, yet there has been no talk of Italy as an enemy country, or of banning Fascist literature.

The second objection to the regulations comes from the necessity of encouraging freedom of thought and speech, especially, in time of war. Are all Communist publications to be regarded as outlawed? If so, what about the scientific study of Communism, a study which must go on, whether Stalin has betrayed his cause or not? The USSR is too big a power in the world to be sent into Coventry. This is proved by the fact that at the present moment Britain is considering a trade treaty with Russia.

It is true that in a country at war there are limits to freedom. Opposition to the war should be checked when it reaches the extreme of disloyalty and active help to the enemy. It is merely childish to suppress all criticism and protest because it is alleged to be disloyal. If the Government were really above criticism the conscience of the nation would not be so uneasy.

There were those who thought that Russia was being given a raw deal.

Letters, T Wright, Trades Hall, Sydney. To this accusation I can only reply that it is untrue. The Communist parties are linked together internationally, but the Russian party (not to be confused with the Soviet Government) has no more right to determine policy than the other parties. The Communist parties, in their respective countries, including our own, are quite capable of finding the correct policy in accordance with our principles.

I challenge Dr Bean to substantiate his statement that Stalin has made declarations supporting Hitler or to show that the Soviet Union has not maintained its policy of neutrality in the present war.

Towards the end of April, the proscribers got a boost as news from Norway leaked out. The Germans had been for years developing the Nazi party in that country, and many of its supporters had got themselves into quite high positions. So that when the Germans invaded, one gentleman, named Quisling, an Army Officer, and well placed within military ranks, used his position to urge the military in Oslo to lay down their arms without resistance.

This consequently earned him great fame as a traitor, and ensured that he would be shot by the Norwegians in 1945. But it also raised the spectre of Australians traitors doing likewise in the event of attack. If the attacker was Russia, the possibility arose that perhaps the Commos here would be as traitorous. This, of course, was stretching things too far, but that scarcely worried the more ardent of the proscribers.

Comment. This was becoming a very controversial subject. At the basis of it was the question of free speech, and how far a person could go before he had to be controlled. Of course, the issue was being muddied by politics, and religion, and patriotism, and ignorance, but that was completely normal. In any case, looking from here, it seemed more than likely that the fierce debate on the matter would continue.

THE ENEMY IS LISTENING

Letters, B Willes. With regard to leakages of news of troop movements for overseas destination, I think the military officer's efforts were misdirected when he laid the blame at the shipping companies' doors. They may be partially responsible, but they are by no means wholly so.

A large percentage of responsibility can be taken by the wives of officers sailing in the various contingents, who cannot bear to hear, without correction, uninformed persons hazarding at sailing dates from observation they make around them day by day.

Very recently speaking to a lad, I inquired if he had heard of his brother's arrival overseas with the last contingent. He replied in the negative, then to my surprise he asked me if I knew the next contingent was sailing on a date he named. I asked him how he knew. "Oh," he replied, "mother works with the officers' wives on a comforts fund, and they told her."

MAY: WAR ON THE WESTERN FRONT

On May 1st, Neville Chamberlain had been Prime Minister of Britain for four years, and during those times he had often received the adulation of the mighty and of the masses. But that was in the past, and it was now almost forgotten, as he was called upon to defend himself and his Government over the fiasco that had developed from his venture into Norway. For the next nine days, his back was right up against the wall, and at the end of that time, fate – in Germanic war dress – intervened, and unceremoniously threw him out of Office.

During the first week of May, Chamberlain was the model of propriety. Here he was, he said, the architect of a splendid military intervention that had seen the defeat and demolition of the German fleet, and then the timely evacuation of 20,000 men to Scotland (without any casualties) when the Southern land forces could not get a bridgehead. Of course, military secrecy demanded that he could give few details, but suffice to say that Britain still had troops in the North of Norway, and this nation had a grim determination that Norway could be sure that British assistance was always available to it.

The trouble was that, at all levels of society, people wanted to know more than that. Everyone in the nation suspected they knew what had happened. It seemed that a British Expeditionary Force of 25,000 men had been sent to Norway. They were too few in number to do the job, they were not trained in fighting or even living in glacial conditions, they had inadequate planes to protect them, and inadequate artillery to support them. The three Branches of the Services were not co-ordinated, the troops had arrived after the Germans so that all of the airfields had already been captured, and they did not have adequate supply lines to help them survive. What people wanted was to be told that these perceptions were wrong, and that in fact they were in the hands of a Government who did know what it was doing, and which could be trusted into the future.

On May 7th, in much heralded Sessions, Chamberlain was due to explain himself to the crowded Houses of Commons and Lords. Such was the build-up to this that in the Commons, the Distinguished Strangers' gallery was indeed distinguished by Ambassadors and Diplomats from France, Argentina, Russia, the US, China, Belgium, Brazil, Egypt, Norway, Sweden, Romania, the Netherlands, Yugoslavia, Bulgaria, and Italy, and the Empire. The Peers gallery was overfull.

None of the above countries were there just to watch the spectacle. They were all vitally concerned, and most of them wondered about their own safety. There were about twenty small nations in the North of Africa, in the Balkans, and in the Middle East that had been relying on Britain and France for protection from the bullies. What were our prospects now, they were asking, if at the first real sign of violence our protectors had packed up and gone home?

THE DEBATE AND AFTER.

Chamberlain, and then his Ministers, added little to his earlier defence. He did point out that Britain's delay in starting action was because Norway had not requested aid, and he was loath to intervene until she did. **This stickler-for-protocol routine** was not at all convincing, not the least because in the few days before landing his forces, the British Navy had spent much time laying mines in Norwegian waters, much to Norway's horror. For two days the Government worked hard to defend its action, but finally a vote showed that its majority in the Commons had fallen drastically to the level where he could not hope to continue.

The population was now convinced that the fault did in fact lie with their Government, and that drastic changes must be made. The Times compiled a post-vote list of the Editorial views of the 14 leading newspapers in Britain, and I have presented four of these below.

Daily Telegraph and Morning Post. The Prime Minister hinted that he was prepared to make changes. He would be well-advised to do so.

News Chronicle. The need of the hour is that Mr Chamberlain should bow to the will of the country, and that a new and strong Government, representative of all the Parties, should be formed without a moment's unnecessary delay.

Daily Mail. It is clear that Mr Chamberlain's Government has lost the confidence of the country. There is only one course. They must resign.

Daily Herald. Parliament has dismissed the PM morally and politically. He was defeated beyond hope of recovery.

It worth noting that these newspapers were normally very supportive of the Conservative Party, and also of Chamberlain. Their muted criticisms disguise much stronger feelings.

The *Sydney Morning Herald*, also normally conservative, was more pointed it its Editorial.

The speeches of the British PM and the Minister for War have left on the public mind an almost terrifying impression of unpreparedness to meet Hitler's blows in Scandinavia, and ineffectiveness in the measures adopted to overtake its consequences. Mr Chamberlain was at pains to repudiate any analogy between Norway and Gallipoli, yet the conclusion is irresistible that the difference is largely one of degree. Blundering and indecision marked both campaigns. The Navy in each case failed to press home its early advantage, and in Scandinavia, as at the Dardanelles, the root cause of disaster appears to have been the same. That is, that operations were regarded as a "sideshow", in this case, important mainly for political reasons, but unworthy of real sacrifices or determined effort.

Fine phrases about "driving the enemy from the hillsides and fjords" and "purging the soil of the Vikings" are no substitute in Ministers for foresight and decision. Wars are won by sound policy translated into resolute action, and not by good intentions. Mistakes must be expected, but Mr Chamberlain has so often proved erroneous in judgement in his dealing with Hitlerism, and belated in action, that confidence in his administration has become dangerously impaired. The nation and the Empire can summon the mighty effort needed for victory only if they are assured they are being firmly and wisely led. At present that assurance is lacking.

Neville Chamberlain spent the night of the 8th of May working hard on staying politically alive, talking to various leaders about possible alliances. But, as it turned out, it was to no avail. Hitler had other things on his mind.

Keep in mind, the recent history of Europe. Austria and Czechoslovakia were almost bloodless acquisitions for Hitler. Then he took Poland, and this was very bloody, and he was kind enough to donate the eastern third of that country to Stalin. After that, Stalin won his war in Lithuania, and then quietly took over its neighbours in Latvia and Estonia. Later, he added Finland to his trophies.

Hitler grabbed Denmark and Norway in April, and that brings us up to date. A lot of territory had been gobbled up, and perhaps you might think that enough was enough. Well, it might be for most people, but not for Hitler. He wanted more.

INVASION OF THE LOW COUNTRIES

At 5am on May 9th 1940, Germany made an all-out attack on her neighbours, Luxemburg, Belgium, and Holland. This was a blitzkrieg invasion, sudden, incredibly rapid, violent, well organised, and well equipped. Luxemburg, a Duchy of only about 30 miles square, immediately capitulated. The other two nations were ready to fight. The trouble for them was that for the last few years they had made military preparations only in a half-hearted way, because they had feared that anything more vigorous would provoke the Germans. Now, of course, they wished they were better prepared, but even 20-20 hindsight can't say for sure they did the wrong thing.

The defence of these countries relied to a large extent on their ability to flood large areas of strategic land, and make it impassable for invaders and their artillery. The trouble with that was that these Germans invaders **flew over** these marshes, and **came in as hordes via parachutes, and on gliders, as well as planes**. Within a couple of days, many forts which were considered impregnable were conquered by the stealth of these troops. The artillery was provided by corps of tanks, and by the never-ending stream of Stukka dive-bombers.

Holland held out for a week. It lost heart when the civilian population in Rotterdam were bombed, and it realised that any air support it could get from the British would not save it from future air raids. Belgium continued to fight on.

The British had a large force, called the British Expeditionary Force of about 400,000 men in the north of France. When the attack came, it was mobilised to move North into Belgium. Within a few days, together with armies of the French, it was fighting, along with the Belgians, against the Germans. Victory in almost ever case went to the Germans.

In the North of France that the British had just left, Hitler unleashed a second army, that eased its way through the "impenetrable" forests of the Ardennes, crossed the "uncrossable" Meuse River, and proceeded toward the coast of France. It took the Allies a few days to work out what was going on, but then they realised that their lines of supply had been cut, and they were potentially in a very nasty trap.

MEANWHILE, BACK IN BRITAIN

The invasion of the Low Countries was the last straw for King George VI, and on that same evening he called Chamberlain, Churchill, and Lord Halifax to Buckingham Palace and formally removed Chamberlain from office.

Somewhat reluctantly he appointed Churchill in his stead. This lucky gentleman thus acceded to the position he had coveted for years, but it was on the day that his troops were moving towards suffering one of the largest defeats in military history.

EVENTS IN BELGIUM AND FRANCE

Towards the end of May, the situation having gotten progressively worse, King Leopold of Belgium surrendered, and left the Allies without valuable support in its lines. As this was happening, the Germans were closing the gap around the coast of France, and the trap was now obvious to all. The BEF and the French decided to retreat, going back over the same territory they had just passed over. As these troops consolidated, they at first formed a pocket of a few hundred miles across, pushed against the coast at Dunkirk. The Germans now came at them from all sides, and from the air, and so the size of this pocket decreased by twenty miles a day.

In the last few days of May, it was decided to evacuate all troops not necessary for the protection of the pocket. A few days later, it was decided to evacuate all troops. So began one of the most remarkable ventures of all time. The beleaguered troops of the BEF were lifted from the beach at Dunkirk by a flotilla of ships and craft of all descriptions, and transported back to England. Many of the vessels were fishing boats, some ferries, many pleasure craft, some under sail rather than power. They were all backed up by lighters, and barges, and ships of the Royal Navy. A total of 338,000 men were thus evacuated and returned safe to British shores.

NOTES ON DUNKIRK.

First. The British people were shocked by the development. In three weeks, the BEF had marched into action, had fought mostly losing-battles, been forced to retreat back to where it started, and been evacuated by a motley collection of often civilian craft. In the process, over 100,000 men had been killed.

Second. The loss of so many men was devastating, but there were also mountains of equipment that were abandoned or destroyed. All the weapons of war, including tanks, trucks, artillery, and ammunition, stores, and everything, were lost to the Army for good.

Third. The evacuation was completed by June 4th, and then the Germans cleared out the last of the pocket, and turned their attention towards the South of France and Paris.

Comment. In writing this account and indeed many others as I progress through these books, I never cease to be affected by the slaughter of so many men, and sometimes civilians, in these battles. I cannot adopt the attitude of military leaders and top politicians who send off troops into battles, knowing full well that many of them will not return. I sympathise with these leaders, and acknowledge that sometimes it might become necessary to do what they are prepared to do. But it is something I could not do, and please believe me when I say this, I grieve every time I so carelessly mention these terrible statistics.

ATTITUDES IN BRITAIN

The evacuation from Dunkirk was not fully known to the British public for a few more days, because of security needs. So Letters here relate to the couple of weeks before that when the Germans had invaded and were being so audaciously successful.

The population was alarmed in all sorts of ways, and knew that something had to be done. The broad range of suggestions show though that there was no unanimity on what that something should be.

Letters, A H Hoare, Ovington Park, near Alresford, Hants. It would seem almost a pity to go to the expense of arming with rifles those members of the Local Defence Volunteers who already have 12-bore shot guns. Many of us know that a 12-bore is a very effective weapon against big game, if it is loaded with well-greased bullets, up to about 75-100 yards.

I would suggest that people who propose to join this corps who own shot guns need only be provided with ammunition. I suppose that it must be ball ammunition.

I would love to take on a Boche parachutist with SSG shot, but fear that a projectile must be of a certain weight to comply with international conventions.

In the dark, when sights are invisible, one wants to throw up one's weapon and shoot fairly accurately, this one can hope to do with a shot gun, made to fit. A rifle is rather a different story, and, if one misses high, one may well kill someone in bed in the next parish but one. This could not happen with a 12-bore gun and greased bullets.

Letters, George Drummond, Northampton. If the warning is sounded two or three cars will at once assemble with the men detailed. Should any parachutists be seen two cars will at once set off. The leading one is to locate the landings and to keep in touch; the other car, when signalled, is to go to the nearest telephone and inform the Chief Constable. Any other cars can be similarly used. Men have also been detailed to "mind" the Post Office.

Some similar scheme can be carried out in every village and town tomorrow. I see no reason why it should not form the nucleus for, and be incorporated in, the official one. It might be the means of rounding up stray or small parties of parachutists before they could get their bearings or gain their objectives.

Letters, A Septuagenarian. Why should there be a limit of age for the Local Defence Volunteers? It is not a question of age, but of physical fitness. There are many men over 65 who are quite fit enough for these part-time semi-domestic patrol duties, and whose knowledge of war, of movement by night, and of the use of arms would more than compensate for any superfluity of years. Let the local commandants have a free hand to enrol any who are physically fit; and if any of us elderly gentlemen get wiped out, we can be better spared than younger men.

Letters, Roy Nash, King's Gardens, Hove. May I suggest that anti-parachutists be armed with Winchester .44 repeating rifles and shotguns using solid "paradox" ball? By this means no extra demand would be made on service rifles and ammunition.

The Winchester is used by professional kangaroo hunters and is very effective at moderate range. Heavy stocks are probably held in America and Canada. As for shotguns, there must be tens of thousands available in this country, and a "paradox" ball will stop big game at short range.

Letters, G Mason, House of Commons. Ought not all Balloon Barrage squads to be armed, if only with shotguns? The balloons seem to provide good protection in cities against low-flying aircraft and parachutists, but one cannot exclude the possibility of treachery, through which they might be rushed by previously concerted efforts, and released. This may seem far-fetched, but so would many of the recent events in Holland, until they took place. A friend of mine who commands a Balloon Squadron in Scotland tells me that several of his squads are in isolated positions, and he has been urging for months that they should be armed. Also, should not Observation Posts throughout the country be armed?

It is a relief to hear that all German males are to be interned, but the net should be spread much wider to include women and other aliens, of whom I am told there are more than 70,000. Temporary hardship may be inflicted on some innocent, and even well-intentioned, persons, but Holland and Norway were ruined from the outset by internal treachery, and we cannot afford to take the slightest risk here.

Letters, Charles Dodson, The Corner House, Caythorpe, Granthan, Lincs. There is little doubt that large numbers of ex-officers of the last War, together with many unemployed retired Regular officers, will rush to enlist in the Local Defence Force. Many such will be in possession of their Service uniforms, and, as in my own case, many will find that their waist-line will still permit the buttoning of their tunics.

Surely, when economy is being preached from high places, these uniforms, ready to step into, should be utilized. All that would be required would be an armlet and the removal of our old rank badges to show that we now had the honour of being full-privates.

Letters, Lilian Faithfull, Four Winds, Birdlip. Is not this the moment to institute universal compulsory training for women on the lines I suggested for men in 1939? Admirable work has been done by women volunteers in the women's voluntary services, and all over the country many women have joined ARP and Red Cross classes and the transport service. But there are, we cannot doubt, many young women who are doing very little and have had no special training. They are still wondering perhaps, what they will do, not being specially trained or drawn to any of the forms of service known to them.

The main difficulty with voluntary workers is that there is an element of instability in the supply which is disturbing to effective production, and, with incomes decreasing in consequence of war taxation, the number of those able to offer voluntary work must diminish, while the demand for various kinds of workers will grow.

Letters, Dorothy Macleod Shute, Sloane Street, SW1. Since the postmen cover most of England from early morning until late in the afternoon, would it not be a good idea to provide them with firearms and train them to use them? Here is a "standing army" already organized, and in an excellent position to deal with emergencies of various kinds if armed. If knowledge of the country is valuable in an emergency, these men have it, and then some!

ATTITUDES IN OZ

People in Australia were as equally disappointed and bewildered as they were in Britain. No one could explain what had happened and why the Germans were able to walk into Holland and Belgium with so little effective opposition. But, like Britain, everyone wanted to do whatever they could, and the suggestions poured out. Again, the remarks are pre-Dunkirk because of censorship.

Letters, R Windeyer KC. In your first leader on Monday last, you referred to the "public anxiety," to "the misgivings that have been felt everywhere," to the "jeopardising" of national unity. But what must be the feelings of Australian British now that Mr Chamberlain has declared himself? More than ever we feel that "anxiety" and those "misgivings": and painfully so, because we cannot make Australia's voice heard in the councils of the Empire.

Australia is already doing much, and as we get into our stride for a "total" effort we shall do more. And shall we have no say in how the war is to be waged? Not only the "national unity" of which you speak, but Imperial unity itself may be shaken unless we share the responsibility and feel that we are respected partners in all vital decisions. Our contribution of effort, as that of Canada and New Zealand, gives a clear right to a seat in an Imperial Council or wherever the ultimate control may be vested. It may be only in the choice of the proper expert.

The recognition of this claim would probably result in a real national Government being formed in England, and even without that, would ensure that the Dominions would contribute a spirit, something different from that of class self-sufficiency and conceit.

Letters, T Rutledge. At the present juncture **it would seem that Australia is lagging in its effort to assist to win the war**. We are fighting with our backs to the wall, recruiting in New South Wales is far short of requirements. I have the utmost faith in the loyalty of the people of Australia, and am convinced that our men of military age are just as willing as they were twenty-five years ago to fight for democracy. Two things are lacking, and I will deal with them separately.

The first is the opportunity to enlist. It is not everyone who owns a motor car or who can afford to buy a railway ticket on the off-chance that after a long wait he may be accepted for service. If accepted he will have to give up certain civil rights in the interests of military discipline, also others which his not-enlisted friend enjoys, such as a glass of beer when his day's work is done. Surely it is time that the recruiting officer came to the recruit (as is traditional), and not demand that the recruit should come to the recruiting officer. In fact, the idea is growing in the country that this is a war by invitation only.

The second is the question of leadership. Last night I listened very carefully to the Prime Minister's speech at 8 o'clock on the wireless. My receiving set is very good and I heard every word. It would have been a most excellent speech from a schoolmaster addressing a class under the age of 14 years.

We must now take the Prime Minister's record. I think I am right in saying that he was one of those who could not conceive that Hitler would make war. Through a series of fortuitous circumstances he became Prime Minister just about the outbreak of war. Is it not time that we followed the example of Great Britain **and appointed a new Prime Minister**?

It appears to me, we in Australia have both in State and Federal spheres a government of the people by **a bureaucracy for a bureaucracy**. Surely it is time that our various Parliaments realised that it would be very much cheaper to hand to the heads of Departments rubber stamps and do away with the cost of the various Legislatures.

Letters, D Lewis. I was amazed to read that the Minister for Aviation says that England should be urged to send aeroplanes to Australia, and the Government here would train the pilots! Surely all the world knows England is desperately outnumbered in men and planes. She has not a plane to spare, with her back to the wall fighting for us; and here we have a man feebly asking for planes. Why is not Australia making planes day and night? What is the matter with the leaders of our people?

Why are there thousands of tons of iron – old engines, rails, boilers, etc – left to rust away, instead of being used for munitions? Why are the races, golf, and sport of all kinds in full swing, while thousands are daily dying for us?

Yet our leaders talk and talk, and have not the moral courage to say we must stop enjoying ourselves. Races must stop; we want the men and the time they spend to work for victory. The people are looking and longing for a man of courage who will throw off red tape and act.

England changed her leaders overnight without an election: why not Australia?

Letters, Soldier's Daughter, Sydney. In England the entire nation has been mobilised. Factories are working seven days a week. Women are taking their places beside their menfolk in many spheres. In Australia the women are eager to serve, but there seems to be no place for them. There are probably others like myself who would willingly face the dangers of the sea voyage to England, and the air raids and dangers of attack, if only they had the necessary finance. England needs the services of every able-bodied man and woman. If the Government remains inactive the women of Australia will demand the right to take their place beside the women of France and Britain.

JUNE: BRITS ON THEIR OWN

In Britain, in the first week of June, the enormity of their loss sank in. The final official figure for the number of men transported from Dunkirk was 338,000, including 113,000 French. The volume of materials left behind or deliberately destroyed was staggering. For example, 75,000 vehicles, 1,200 field guns, and 11,000 machine guns.

The nation's leaders were deliberate in what they said about the debacle. Their utterances described the heroism of the men, their gallantry, and their magnificent fight against overwhelming odds. Understandably, they were careful not to recognise officially that there had been a terrific defeat, and used stirring words to give solace to the population. Churchill talked about "Never surrender" and promised that "we shall not flag or fail." Many distinguished members of Government pointed out that this retreat was just one battle, and that Britain would come back, and win in the long run.

But, it seems, their words were scarcely needed. The vast majority of the population had no intention at all of giving up, and instead were firmed in their resolve that the nation would not stop fighting until Hitler was defeated. That, however, was before the events in France in the next two weeks, and at the end of the month, their resolve would be tested again.

THE BATTLE FOR FRANCE

While the Allied forces were making their escape from Dunkirk, Hitler was continuing his victorious drives. He ordered his troops to move South and, right across France, made a rapid advance. In two weeks, his forces were ready to occupy Paris. The French Government declared this an "open city", which meant that French troops would vacate it, and not defend it, and therefore, not destroy it. So Paris was occupied peacefully on June 14. A few days later, the new French Government under Marshall Petain sued for an armistice, and this was duly signed on June 22nd. **France was out of the War**, and Britain was fighting Hitler all by herself.

Under the Armistice, the new Government would rule France, in collaboration with the Germans, from the city of Vichy. This was plotted to be a co-operative government, with France as the junior partner. Under the propaganda of Goebbels, the two nations were to march hand-in-hand into an era of enlightenment and prosperity. But, importantly in the immediate future, it meant that Paris and Vichy France were spared the brutality of occupation that Hitler often dished out to the lands he conquered.

A few points to note. Firstly, as the Germans approached Paris, about 10 million people, fearing that brutality, packed up and left home, and went south. Most of them had nowhere to go, they just thought it would be better elsewhere than with the dreaded Hun.

> Every aspect of this incredible panic was revealed in the fleeing cars which were filled, almost to the point of breaking their axles, with the most disparate collection of stuff, screaming females, males in shirt sleeves, dripping with sweat, eyes bulging, purple necks, reduced within an hour to the condition of Neolithic brutes, young virgins with their blouses completely open, mothers-in-law half-dead from shock and fatigue, little doggies in their own filth, piles of furs, quilts,

boxes of jewellery, containers of camembert, fetish-dolls...

Second. The German occupation of Paris, and the subsequent occupation, was a very civilised affair. Hitler had issued orders that his troops behave themselves on all occasions. Within a few days, the German soldiers were seen everywhere in cafes sipping coffees, paying for their purchases and being nice to orphans and widows. Hitler himself spent two days sightseeing Paris, and issued orders that the city should remain the centre of European culture.

Third. The new French Government had decided on the Armistice. The people did not know whether to laugh or cry. None of them wanted war, and the Armistice removed any worry about this, and about their nation being pillaged. On the other hand, they had been expecting to fight to the finish, and perhaps winning and conquering the Nazis. Now they had to suffer, or perhaps not suffer, German domination in a velvet glove. Perhaps, most of them thought, it might work out. In any case, what could any one person do?

Fourth. Many millions who had fled Paris now returned. Some few of them, mainly the ambitious ones, became active collaborators with the Nazis. Most people became passive, and only a few remained active opponents of the new regime.

This was a period which, after a few years, French people were happy to forget. Some thought that the French had signed for a shameful peace, while other would shrug and ask what else could they have done. But in any case, as the dust slowly cleared, it became apparent that many men would be recruited to fight for the German army, against the nation that they had so staunchly supported just a few weeks earlier.

Fifth. Signor Mussolini could wait no longer. He dived headlong off the fence, and declared war on the Allies on June 11th. His divisions of troops attacked the French troops in the South of France, around the Alps, and hoped to over-run and capture a large area of France, literally, and never give it up. Alas for him, his troops were not really keen on fighting their long-term neighbours, and made almost no progress. So when the Armistice was signed about a week later, he had nothing to show for his meagre effort, and he made none of the territorial gains he had long coveted. Still, he was now in the war and, as we shall see, his navy in the Mediterranean, and his troops in North Africa, proved significant at times in the future.

THE FALL OF FRANCE: A BRITISH VIEW

The British were astounded by the withdrawal of France. Frederick Bloomsfield of Hull expressed the situation clearly.

> I find it hard to accept and even harder to explain the abject surrender and capitulation of the French nation. Britain and France have for years been allies, we have dozens of agreements that say we will fight together, and stick together to the very end. Only a few weeks ago, half the British army was in France, showing we were willing to fight for that nation, and preserve its freedom. Yet as soon as aggression came, as soon as the Hun and the dreaded Dago threw their troops against us, France pulled out of the War, and left us to our own devices. Is this perfidy, or betrayal, or cowardice?

It is all very well to say, as many people do, that France was betrayed by a handful of leaders, and that the people were opposed to the Armistice. But where is the evidence of this? There is none. The people and the Army are simply accepting the situation, and preparing to become an ally of Germany, and probably, in their hopeful moments, expecting to share in the benefits when Britain is gobbled up by the Nazi menace.

Well let me tell them something. Britain will not be gobbled up. We will fight the forces of evil and destroy them. France has betrayed us in the most callous way, leaving us to bear the burden of preserving freedom all by ourselves. If in the course of doing that, we must deliver justice to the nation that so betrayed us, we will do so without hesitation.

OZ NEWS AND VIEWS

In Australia, too, people were bewildered by the turn of events. At the start of the month, they could scarcely believe that the British Army had been routed at Dunkirk. As the month progressed, they watched in daily dismay as the French were chased back to Paris and beyond. Then came the signing of the Armistice taking France into some kind of neutrality, and with it came the possibility that French Forces might even be used to fight the Brits and the Empire. It was all beyond comprehension.

Once again, the newspapers were absolutely flooded with Letters and Editorials crying out in frustration that somehow we should do something. Mr Menzies, and his Cabinet, were often the targets of forceful suggestions.

Letters, M Witts. To say that the British Empire – and with it our own land – is in peril, is but to repeat what has been said many times during the past fateful week. Britain realised her position, and acted promptly by replacing the gentle but indecisive Mr Chamberlain with a man of action – one who not only sees what should be done but insists on that thing being done.

We in Australia are faced with a similar position – a too-easy-going Prime Minister, and it is time that we woke up to the fact. Mr Menzies has not that driving force so essential to leadership in these perilous times. He is a fine speaker; but words will not turn back those hordes of raging Germans from the Channel ports. A man who, at a time when he should be straining every nerve to aid the Allies, and at the same time make our own defence more complete – can spend valuable time "considering" and finally "approving" an extravagant labour-diverting scheme to manufacture motor cars in Australia, cannot, by any stretch of imagination be called a suitable war-time Prime Minister.

Admittedly that office, in times like the present is not an easy one to fill, but with our population of seven million surely a man of the calibre of W M Hughes can still be found to lead us.

Letters, J Hardie. The reasoned and resolute utterances of Mr Menzies have ensured him the support of the great majority of Australians. Where, in or outside Parliament, is there a man with half his ability and force of character? The criticisms of our war effort are as unreasonable as inept. Australia, as a nation, is organised for peace, profit, and pleasure, and it was impossible to put it on a war footing, armed, equipped, and organised, in the few weeks since we realised the deadly danger that Australia and the world are in.

Mistakes have been made; they must not be made again. There has been inefficiency: we must weed out the inefficient. But let us not carp at those who are striving to the limits of their capacity to make Australia safe.

Letters, W McIntosh. Mr Menzies calls to the enemy that "If you want us, come and get us" – yet he is concerned with the building of motor cars. If the battle flag of the Empire be lowered, it will not be motor cars we will need, but shrouds. Every loyal subject should raise a united voice for a virile leader and a national Government. The Empire needs it now.

OUTBACK OZ

The farmers and graziers throughout the land were also waiting anxiously for guidance.

Letters, Harold Simpson, Glen Innes. One of the most demoralising factors in the community today is the feeling of utter lack of direction. Nowhere is this more so than in our primary industries, where this feeling of uncertainty and unrest is undoubtedly causing great inefficiency, as well as much misguided effort.

At present, individuals produce what they consider most appropriate without any real guide as to what is in the best interests of the

Empire and her Allies in the colossal struggle ahead. There is danger of over-production of many products, which would become a drug on the local market, and be of no benefit to the Empire or her Allies, while there may be a shortage of other products that would be invaluable if available to ship overseas. At any time this would be a waste of effort and economic loss, but at a time like the present it would be a national calamity.

The source of vast quantities of Britain's food supplies has fallen into enemy hands; all of these foods can be produced here to abundance if required. It was believed that unlimited quantities of butter would be required from Australia. There now appears to be some doubt of this, owing to the enormous use of margarine. What a waste of national effort if this butter is to be produced only to find it is not wanted, when that effort could be directed into other and more profitable channels.

In most of our closely settled districts we can turn from the production of one product to another at very short notice, but the urgent requirement is: "Give us guidance."

THE FEDS ACTS ON COMMUNISTS

Another piece of legislation that passed without comment was one that **out-lawed the Communist Party**. In peace time, this would have caused a furore. But in these days of near-panic, no one – apart from a small handful of Reds – seemed at all concerned.

ITALIANS IN OZ

When Italy declared war on June 11, the various State and Commonwealth and Army authorities that had been planning for this, leapt into action. One day later, thousands of Italians were in custody. This included many who were already naturalised. Over 1,000 shops, where refreshments, drinks, fruit, and fish and chips, had been sold by Italians, were closed, and within a day, every Italian Club and organisation would be also be shut.

It was expected that many of the persons would "soon" be released, after processing, and only those who were regarded as a possible menace, because of known Fascist or anti-British views, would be interned. It was the largest round-up operation in Australia's history. One man whose house had been raided was found to be in possession of a still. He was fined twenty Pounds, and the still was confiscated and taken to the Police Station.

Comment. The act of swooping on Italians, many of them naturalised, in the middle of the night and dragging them away from their families, passed almost un-noticed in the Press and Letters. The *SMH* only recorded a few Letters on the subject, and these scarcely come to terms with the broad issue of the freedoms that we were fighting overseas to protect.

> **Letters, An Old Woman.** As an English woman who went through the war of 1914-18, I should like to suggest that alien enemies, one and all, be transported from the country. Surely, there are some islands belonging to Australia where they could be sent until after the war.
>
> Give them food to carry on for a time until they could grow enough food, from seed supplied

them. Further, supply tools for them to cultivate the land. If an enemy attacked us, would signing a paper kill in the alien the love of his native land?

Letters, J Preston. If the Commonwealth has the authority to close Italian shops, surely it has the power to remove the stocks and give them to some charitable institution or send them out to our troops in camp, instead of permitting large stocks of fruit and vegetables to lie and rot in the shops that have been closed.

OTHER EUROPEAN NEWS

Last month, Luxemburg, Holland and Belgium fell to the Huns, and this month, all of France did as well.

But, you are not finished yet. In the last few days of June, Russia, obviously feeling a bit left out, took over half of the Baltic State of Romania. This was a bloodless coup, and tightened Red control over the Black Sea.

SOME CEREMONIAL WISDOM.

Letters, W Charge, MBE, Royal Society of St George. Tomorrow is St George's Day. It also is the birthday and death day of the immortal Shakespeare. Let us not then be ashamed on "England's Day" to wear the rose – the beautiful emblem of England which for centuries has been so inextricably interwoven with the history of our nation.

At Home, and in those Englands beyond the seas, many branches of the Royal Society of St George have been established and seek to encourage the general observance of "England's Day" working side by side in amicable emulation with the kindred societies of St Andrew, St Patrick, and St David. There never was a time in our national history when devoted patriotism to the Motherland was more imperative than today. Too much latitude has been allowed to those in Australia who see fit to belittle and abuse the Empire and to disseminate political doctrines designed to submit all loyalty to the Crown and all national sentiment as well.

In this connection, we cannot do too much to bring into our public education that sincere love of country on which the whole structure of our national existence depends. In Germany, Russia and Italy, immense populations have grown to manhood imbued with fanatical attachments to political and racial doctrines, fanned and intensified by all the acts of unlimited and well-planned propaganda. It is, therefore, folly to leave our own people unaided to work out for themselves, in a species of mental anarchy, some irresponsible and ill-conceived philosophy of living, acquired hugger-mugger from the spate of false and confusing doctrines.

The loss of liberty and personal rights in ravaged countries occasioned by the bullying of our enemies, aided by traitors within, must bring us back to an appreciation of all that our long accustomed liberties and privileges means to our own people. Let us fight to ensure that knowledge and love of country shall be the themes, not only of our national education, but also of our everyday actions – and in our homes.

Comment. In reviewing Letters, I often note that those written in 1940 are much more eloquent than the quick notes we all now write as email. The above Letter is a good example of that eloquence. Remember, such Letters were almost certainly written long-hand with a pen and ink under a 40-watt globe. Quite a task.

QUESTIONS ON SHEEPSKINS

Letters, Commissioner, Sydney. There is a body of people preparing sheepskin waistcoats for our soldiers abroad, and asking people to subscribe for this object. Apparently they have not heard that the waistcoats were an absolute failure in the last war for the reason that they were the harbour for countless vermin which could not be destroyed. The wiser plan would be to make **leather waistcoats for the soldiers.**

AN INTERESTING LAW REPORT

The High Court dismissed the appeal of Anne Furlong, who had applied to have the licence for the Oaks Hotel at Sydney's Neutral Bay transferred to her. Miss Furlong, a single woman, had applied as the executrix of her mother's will. It was agreed by the Court that Miss Furlong was of good character, and highly suitable as a licensee.

The Crown submitted that she was in fact **unsuitable because she was unmarried**. It said that the Liquor Act of NSW provided that "no such applicant shall be entertained where such applicant is an unmarried woman (not being a widow)." There were some exceptions to this Clause, but the Crown argued that she did not fit into any of these. In a two-to-one decision, the Court found that Miss Furlong should **not** be granted the licence.

JULY: THE BATTLE OF BRITAIN BEGINS

The Brits were bewildered. Six weeks ago they felt secure in the knowledge that they were protected by two magnificent Armies, and were just about ready to crack the vile oppressor on the Continent. Now, suddenly, one of these Armies, their own, had been routed and forced to flee from France.

Then the second Army, the French, had surrendered to the Nazis after only two weeks of fighting. What had happened to the Maginot Line, and what had happened to the might of the British forces? Could it be that the Germans might right now continue on their winning way, and hop across the Channel and lay waste to England? Could the British forces protect the nation, or would they again give way before the miraculous might of Hitler?

Fortunately, Hitler knew that he could not do this. He was not prepared for such a huge effort, he did not have the ships to make the crossing of the Channel, and if he did, he would have been straffed to death by the RAF on their home turf. In fact, what he wanted was for the British to sue for peace.

Over the first three weeks of July, he set his ambassadors to work suggesting in varying places he would give generous peace terms to the British if they came to the table, and then on July 20th he made a formal approach to Britain. It took Churchill about a week to respond in the negative, and then he, and a number of his Ministers including Lord Halifax, made it clear that Britain would fight on, and would never rest until Hitler and Nazism had been fully defeated.

In the meantime, Churchill had not been idle. On July 5th, the Royal Navy had sailed into the Algerian harbour at Mers-el-Kebir, and **sunk forty per cent of the French fleet**. This fleet had departed from French ports as the Germans advanced, and were sitting round scratching their heads about what the future held for them.

Churchill provided the answer for many of them by sinking them, often with large numbers of men on them. At the same time, another twenty per cent of the French fleet capitulated to the British over in Alexandria on the far East of the Mediterranean. Thus a total of sixty per cent of the above-surface French fleet was out of commission for the War, and that fleet now posed no further problems. After the German loss in Norway, only the excellent Italian navy had to be reckoned with. Except, that is, for the Japanese, who no one worried about.

BATTLE READY

Hitler was active in that same meantime. He reasoned that if the British rejected his peace overtures, he would simply invade the nation and take it by force. To do this, he concocted his plan for Operation Sea Lord, which called for **the occupation of England to start the middle of September.**

The first stop in this Operation was to gain control of the Channel, and the Channel ports, and the hinterland near them. So, in mid July, he started bombing raids on those targets, with massive numbers of planes flying night and day and delivering loads up and down the coast. This was the first of **three phases in the Battle of Britain**, and it lasted till the middle of August. Most Britishers did not know at the time that this was the prelude to invasion, and thought that the higher level of bombing was simply part of Hitler's aim to demoralise them.

THE FUTURE BATTLE AGAINST RUSSIA

Hitler just had to keep busy, so he occupied himself for the rest of July nutting out a plan to attack and invade and occupy **his current ally, Russia**. He called his military leaders together on July 27th and informed them of his intention to invade Russia in May 1941, and ordered them to make ready. His officers thought he was crazy, because he would then, in all probability, be exposed to fighting on both the Eastern and Western Fronts. Not at all deterred, he set the plan in concrete, and turned back to Britain.

TWO TYPICAL LETTERS

> **Letters, A Country Parson.** You stated today that "the quiet resolution of the British people is based on a knowledge of the situation and of their own strength." But in my constant parish visiting I find it is based on something much more real and certain than any knowledge of the national situation.
>
> In fact, judging from the numerous questions put to me daily, there is great ignorance both of the situation and of our power to meet it. But there is an almost amazing faith, not only in God, but also in the determination of our leaders to see that right shall conquer in the end. Country cottage folk, in this danger zone, go about their daily tasks calmly and cheerfully, without panic and without fear, and certainly without idle boasting or despair.
>
> I am convinced that British steadfastness at this critical time is based rather on character

and faith than on any real knowledge of material facts. And the nearness of danger in no way disturbs this solid mental calm.

Letters, V Stack. A considerable number of children have recently left from this grant-aided school to travel overseas under one of the private schemes so bitterly criticised by Labour MP's.

As the headmistress of such a school I can therefore speak with some impartiality on the whole question of overseas evacuation, and I should like to say how grossly unfair seems to me the attacks upon the "well-to-do" parents for accepting the chance of sending their children to safety. Those who resent their action, and, feel "bitter and angry" when they see photographs of these children in the newspapers, are both ungenerous and illogical. Parents do not decide upon separation from their children without much stress of mind, and this distress should be increased by unjust insinuations against them seems to me intolerable.

THE BATTLE OF BRITAIN STARTED

Typical News Item. The Air ministry announced this morning that the latest reports now show that nine more enemy aircraft – two bombers and seven fighters – were destroyed during Saturday's air battles round our coasts by fighters of the RAF, and by AA batteries. This brings the total number of enemy aircraft shot down on Saturday to 21. Eighteen of these were brought down by our fighters, and three by AA guns. Our fighters intercepted and shot down an enemy fighter off the coast yesterday afternoon. This was the third during the day.

An earlier communiqué stated that air fights began in the early hours and went on all day. Several other raiders are known to have been severely damaged. The pilot of one of our fighters which was lost is safe. The biggest engagement of the day was when 35 enemy aircraft took part in a battle off the South-East Coast on Saturday evening. Dive bombers attacked a convoy, but were driven off by a shattering fire from warships and shore batteries, though salvos of bombs fell round the ships. A series of dog fights were seen, and several of the Germans appeared to have been damaged.

Seventeen German bombers made a lightning attack on ships in a South of England harbour in the afternoon, but hit none. They were driven off by anti-aircraft fire and engaged by British fighters over the Channel. Earlier in the day fighters accounted for one raider intercepted over Scotland and another which landed in South-Eastern England. The four occupants of the second machine were taken prisoner.

Another Typical News Item. Some persons were killed and two injured by nine or 10 bombs dropped by a single raider on a town in North-West England yesterday. Two targets were selected by the bomber when it dived; one was a school, and on and around the school four or five bombs were dropped. The school was wrecked and houses in neighbouring streets suffered considerable damage. Though the target was a densely populated part of a town, the loss of life was surprisingly small; and there were some remarkable escapes.

After a bomb hit a small hotel in North-East England while the occupants were asleep, a demolition squad rescued many of them from beneath the debris. Occupants who took refuge under the stairs were unhurt. Bombs damaged a house and a factory making tin boxes, but in both places there were no serious casualties.

The crew of an enemy bomber which was shot down by fighters in South-West England yesterday afternoon were captured by Captain Phillips, a member of the LDV, who was motoring with his son, a private in the RAMC. The son attended to the injuries of the pilot and navigator. Captain Phillips said that when he saw the machine come down he put on his LDV armlet, and flourishing a revolver, ran to the bomber. "Two of the men were wounded," he said, "and they had already been pulled clear by the third German airman. The men offered no resistance. They were disarmed, and after their injuries had been attended they were taken off by a military detachment."

OZ NEWS AND VIEWS

Bob Menzies and his Government were due to face the electorate by December, at the latest. At this moment in July, they were not impressing the voters. In particular, their handling of the war effort was constantly under attack. This was a situation in which **a really good government might have starred**, they might have done everything right, in a big hurry, and got the entire nation mobilised into a fantastically productive society.

This however was not such a government. It had fallen down to an extent in all of these things, and was just muddling along, as fast as it was capable. Of course it would be easy to argue that no government in a democracy could do all that was needed in the circumstances, and that only a totalitarian ruler could achieve the desirable miracles. But such arguments were not acceptable excuses, so Bob and his men were fighting for votes.

A NEW OFFENSIVE MEASURE

They did not help themselves here by introducing a new Regulation that got a lot of people offside. This was issued under the Nation Security Act, passed last week, and gave extraordinary powers to the Director-General of the Department of Information, Sir Keith Murdoch. This body, created to provide propaganda and to implement censorship, was given sweeping controls over information flows, such as "absolute power to **compel any newspaper** or periodical to publish any statement or material supplied by the D-G in whatever position is required and without limit in respect of the space supplied." Other draconian measures were set forth, and similar restrictions were placed on radio and cinema.

Outrage was the order of the day. It was no use saying that there was an expectation that the powers would rarely be used. The *SMH* answered this with "the powers are there, and experience has shown all too clearly that excessive authority placed in political and bureaucratic hands is very liable sooner or later to be used." It went on to point out that "to date, co-operation and good sense of all concerned has allowed self-censorship to operate without noticeable friction or abuse of authority" and such a working system was now to be replaced by a dictatorship over the Press and other instruments of publicity.

Letters opposing the new regulations were prolific. For example:

> **Letters, Reginald Lloyd.** The arbitrary powers given to Sir Keith Murdoch undoubtedly represent a tribute to the abilities of an extremely capable man, but they also constitute a tremendous blow to the accepted independence of thought

of the Australian people. I doubt if any other among the many eminent leaders of journalism would have accepted powers which implied the right to dragoon the Australian mind.

There exists today an adequate censorship. Its scope enables it to prevent publication of subversive or foolish material. But it has not the right to present a manufactured view point, and no matter how desirable it may appear to officialdom, it is an arrogation of rights which can only be regarded as despotic, to place the Press, radio, and movie screen at the disposal of a propaganda Director.

I have no doubts of Sir Keith's honesty of purpose, but I will resolutely refuse to listen to Department of Information radio propaganda, to read newspaper material from the same source, or to watch screen material of Department of Information origin. This is not because I am indifferent to it, but because I count it my duty as a free Australian to resist an administrative dictatorship. As it turns out the activities of the Department, or the broadcasting stations, have been lamentably injudicious already.

Letters, David Ferguson. It is not my purpose to discuss the Regulations, except to say that I can conceive cases in which they might usefully be applied. I hope the occasion will never arise, but if at any time it may arise it is wise to have provision made in advance for dealing with it. The Government was given power to make regulations of this kind because we trusted it to apply them honestly and loyally for the sole purpose for which it was given – to secure the public safety, the defence of the Commonwealth, and the efficient prosecution of the war. Let us continue the trust we have put in the Government – not the Menzies Government, but whatever Government may be in power during the war, whether it is led by Mr Menzies, Mr Curtin, Mr Beasley, or anybody else to whom the nation chooses to confide its destinies. If we cannot, then it is a poor outlook for Australia.

Letter, B Smyth. The thing that worries me about the new Regulations is that only last week the Government brought down the new National Security Act, and told us that it would probably never use it. Just one week later it brings down these Regulations under the Act, and tells us again that it might never use them.

Well, they have already used the Act. Can we trust them not to use the Regulations? And in any case, someone tell me why these instruments are enacted at all if they will never be used. The Government should go away and think what it is they really want to control, and legislate against that. Simply to fire a shotgun at everything is not good enough.

Comment. Despite Mr Ferguson's sober thoughts, the bulk of the Letters opposed the legislation. The Government made matter worse by making another way-out proposal, seeking more extreme powers.

POSTPONE THE ELECTIONS

Mr Menzies, at the end of July, proposed that legislation be introduced **to allow the Government to postpone the upcoming elections** if the need arose. His proposal was that the option would not necessarily be used, but should be available if it was required. The enabling legislation would need to be passed in the two Houses or be approved by a national referendum.

Comment. This was a controversial and cunning suggestion. The immediate response of most Members of Parliament was one of shock that such a prolongation could be contemplated. But many of them quickly wavered, realising that it meant that they would stay in their seats for another year or so, and not have to face the electorate.

Letters, Frank Louat, Constitutional Assn of NSW. The executive of the Constitutional Association considers that, apart from special circumstances making it impracticable, the holding of a Federal election is vital to the national war effort. It is obvious to everyone that public opinion in Australia still lacks the unity of outlook which has been established in Britain. The essential condition of achieving this unity is an appeal to the people so that electors of all parties can feel that they have made their own war-time choice of leaders and spokesmen.

The present proposal appears to be that the Federal Parliament should be given an unfettered discretion to decide whether its own term should be extended. In our opinion this is a gravely unsatisfactory course to adopt.

It is necessary to speak plainly. My executive has little faith in the judgment of any elected assembly on the question of when its own term should come to an end. During the 1914-18 war, the Homan Government lengthened the life of the State Parliament for reasons which may have seemed better to the politicians than they did to the electors.

The truth of the matter is that we are not at war in the same sense as Britain is at war. In any case, Britain is not seeking any such powers. We still have our Constitution to preserve the most precious safeguard of our rights, and until we come face-to-face with a real emergency, we must guard those rights against all further encroachments.

Letters, H Malden. A coalition Government without the people's confidence should not be imposed on Australia. Mr Menzies apparently would rather change the Constitution than face the electors. How could such a Ministry hold the people's confidence and co-operation?

Canada recently held a general election and went back to power much stronger, having the people's mandate. War effort doubled in no time.

The present Ministry is the fifth in one Parliament. Surely it is high time the people exercised their Constitutional right at the elections, after so much shuffling and changes of Ministries, and all that that means. A newly elected Parliament would stop all this dissension in political circles. The present Parliament is no longer recognisable as the one elected in 1937.

Letters, Unity At Any Cost. An election at this critical time would be foolish in the extreme. It would do more than engender the old party spirit, so much to be deplored, especially at this time, and would not by any means return us a government any better to deal with the war effort than the present one. It would be only playing into the hands of the Labour Party, and create a political disturbance most disastrous to Australia at the present time.

ALIENS IN AUSTRALIA

The status of aliens was by no means certain. Some had been interned, and were sent to camps. Some had been interned and released. Some persons who had been naturalised were interned, and again, some were not. Many migrants who had fled here from repression in Germany or Poland wanted to join the Services but were not allowed to. The legal provisions were different from State to State, and the Federal authorities often said different things from the State police and from the Army. It was great mess.

The *SMH* addresses the issue with force. "If any person from an enemy country, or Britain, are guilty of sedition, or constitute a danger to the public interest, they should be interned without fear or favour. But as a matter of principle, nothing could be more indefensible than to break the implicit pledge of civilised treatment which Australia gave the refugees by offering them a haven. We cannot subject them to a second repression, and by letting **hysteria take the place of reason**, then betray the very cause of justice and humanity for which we are fighting. Conduct so reprehensible should not be tolerated in this State or Commonwealth."

Letters, J McCallum. The proposal to intern all "enemy aliens" is highly controversial. The case for it is that people who might be spies or conspirators would be put where they can do no harm.

The people who plead that case have neither supported it by sufficient evidence nor answered the case against it. They have not explained what the term "enemy alien" means, or done anything to enlighten the public regarding the real danger presented by the enemy in our midst.

"Enemy alien" is merely a technical term. It includes Nazis and Fascists who are the deadliest enemies of the British Commonwealth, and also decent Germans, Austrians, and Italians, who hate tyranny as much as we do. The proposal to "intern them all" means that we lump our best friends with our worst foes.

But if we put all people legally described as "enemy aliens" behind barbed wire, what have we done for our security? Possibly caught a spy or two, who might be better outside, for then our intelligence service could watch their activities and learn something of the real Nazi infiltration network – and certainly embittered many potential good citizens. And outside would still be the Fifth Column – the people who think that Democracy is a failure, that Hitler is a strong man, who saved Germany from Bolshevism – and would have saved us, if we hadn't been so foolish as to quarrel with him – that the working men must be coerced into supporting the Empire, that this country needs a dictator, that Mussolini really doesn't want to hurt us, that General Franco is a "Christian gentlemen," and so on – ad nauseum.

Representatives of the old Diggers should leave all controversial issues alone – except when they speak in their private capacity as ordinary citizens. Tolerance was the outstanding characteristic of the old AIF. We hit hard, hated nobody, and left the fostering of the proper degree of public animosity to others. Let us still follow that sound tradition.

Letters, A Wyatt. It is with extreme disquiet that one reads the words of the Premier Mair on the subject of "enemy aliens." In this time of world chaos, surely we have the right to expect in our leaders the qualities of courage, strength, and vision. Yet here, at the very time when the strength of unity is being emphasised, we find our Premier urging, in effect, that the stand taken in this matter by our Prime Minister is mistaken and unsafe.

Included in the vast taxes which the public shoulders so uncomplainingly are we not paying substantially for an Intelligence Department, whose duty it is to investigate every individual who could, by any possibility, come under suspicion? Does our Premier wish us to draw the inference that this Government Department is inefficient, and a waste of public funds?

Does Mr Mair repudiate the permission granted by the Federal Government to these harried people to cross the world, and risk their last remaining resources in the hope of finding peace and liberty here, where we are so given to boasting of both?

Much is being said just now about fighting for the survival of Christianity, and also of the emergence of a better world ideal from the darkness of war. If there were any shred of sincerity in all this spate of words we have only to question our own hearts as to what we think Christ would have done for a wronged and suffering people.

Admittedly, there may be a sprinkling of spies among those who have sought refuge here, but I, for one, have sufficient confidence in our intelligence officers to leave that small proportion to them. I shall not have confidence to pray for victory if I have helped, in blind panic, to stone the desperate suppliant at our gate.

Letters, Curt Prerauer. The progress of Jewish persecution, was more gradual in Germany. Those, like myself, who were dismissed from their profession in 1933, and came to Australia early have been able to become naturalised.

Others were not so fortunate. They were admitted only much later, many obstacles being put in their way. They were deprived of all their possessions, their businesses taken from them, their money confiscated. A few of them have succeeded, against great odds, in establishing themselves in this country. Others are struggling very hard to earn a living – all this, because they were tormented physically and mentally by Hitler and his minions and were glad to escape with their lives.

It is hardly likely that such people, who were not even considered as Germans after Hitler's ascendancy, should participate in treacherous activities. If anyone has cause to desire the downfall of Germany it is they. Surely, they ought not to be made to suffer as "enemy aliens," for the simple reason that the five years have not yet elapsed before they may apply for naturalisation.

WHAT'S HAPPENING TO MUSIC?

Letters, B Rothwell. I heartily agree with Mr Hay's proposal to hold weekly concerts and so give our talented locals a chance, and also the public a feast of melody and harmony.

It is appalling that so many young people (and some of the older ones too) are lacking in musical taste and knowledge (unless music students) and seem to be quite satisfied with **noise and motion, and call it modern music**. We should strive to bring about a musical revival and so help them to appreciate really good music. I know how difficult it is for a local composer or performer to be recognised unless some influential person can boost one, and that luck does not come to all.

For years I have tried to get theatrical managers to look at an operetta, purely Australian, and most suitable for pantomime, but so far have not been successful because it is an Australian composition, and they don't know whether it is good, bad, or indifferent; so time marches on, and year after year they give the public the same old pantomimes. Why is it?

Comment. Mr Rothwell would be appalled by what has happened to music since he wrote.

AUGUST: THE BATTLE HOTS UP

At the start of August, all of Britain knew that they were slowly approaching a crisis. Everyone was aware that the worst that could happen would be that the Germans might invade in a few weeks, and that Britain would be forced to its knees, with a considerable loss of life and property. The best that could happen, realistically, was that the Nazis would try to invade and fail, and go away and never try again. In between, there were a host of possibilities, and if there were 40 million people in Britain, there were also 40 million opinions.

Hitler, through his newspapers and his radio broadcasts and his speeches, made it clear that he now intended to invade. He had already started to soften up the country with the first phase of the Battle of Britain, his raids on the Channel shipping and its environs. As well, his military was preparing for Operation Sea Lord, and even though the **detail** of this was invisible to the Brits, it was common knowledge that it was all happening on a grand scale.

So August opened with more of the bombings that had marked the end of July, but every day Hitler threw more and more planes into the attack. Down they came to the South of England in squadrons of 60 bombers, or sometimes 100, supported by fighters for protection, and dropped their bombs on their targets. The RAF fighters rose up to destroy them, the ack-ack guns pounded away at them, balloon barrages confounded them, and searchlights pin-pointed them at night. As the month went on, they got more daring, and tried more daylight raids. It might have seemed that Britain was in a hopeless position, except for **three saving factors**.

The first saving factor was that this was not just one-way traffic. Britain had developed long-range bombers that could fly all the way to western Germany, and even to Berlin, and while the Germans were bombing the Channel ports, the Brits were dishing out an equal share to the industrial centres and airfields in Germany.

The second saving factor was that the Brits were getting the better of the air battles that were developing. Despite the inflated numbers given by both sides, it was clear that the Germans were losing twice as many planes as the British. And as the weeks went on, these numbers were becoming alarming, more especially to the Germans.

They had started this Battle with more aircraft than the Brits. But the Brits were now turning out planes from their factories much faster that the Germans. On top of that, the Americans were also coming to the party, and providing enough planes to make a difference. So the Brits were wiping out their initial deficit, and heading for a lead. Add to that the new British fighter planes, the Spitfire and the Hurricane, were superior fighting craft, and it was becoming apparent that the longer the Battle went on, the less desperate Britain's position became.

The third saving factor was the British people themselves. Whether they were the Servicemen fighting the Battle, or civilians hundreds of miles away, or politicians in London, the population was united in its determination that Britain should not be conquered, and that it was up to everyone to do everything he could to avoid that fate. There was a grim determination across the population, a matter-of-factness that said we will survive despite all odds, that was in stark contrast to the vacillation and uncertainty of the French a month earlier. As the weeks wore on, and

Sea Lord went through its phases, the British remained undaunted, and withstood some dreadful moments, and were always ready for more. This nation was resolved, as if a single entity, not to succumb.

For the first half of August, Phase One went on, with increasing ferocity. It came to the crunch on August 17, when the Germans lost a reported 169 planes in the one day. When such losses were weighed up against the damage that was being inflicted, it became obvious that attacks should be directed to other types of targets. Air raids were halted for about a week, but in the last week of August, activity started up again, and Phase Two was under way. This lasted just two to three weeks, until September 7th, and was designed to put the RAF out of action, and at the same time, if it involved the bombing of cities on the Southern coastline, then that was a bonus.

The Germans now changed from attacks on shipping and ports to attacks on aircraft and landing fields, with huge air battles being fought over wide areas. Headlines tell the story:

RAIDERS OVER LONDON ALL NIGHT.

27 AERODROMES AND OIL PLANTS ATTACKED.

GREAT AIR BATTLES IN LONDON AREA.

650 RAIDING AIRCRAFT TURNED BACK.

But, in an ominous sign, the Southern and South Eastern cities such as Folkestone, Essex, Sussex, Kent, and Portsmouth, were being bombed more and more. This was not carpet bombing, but the level had lifted from the occasional bomb to induce terror, up to deliberate targeting of factories and railways and the like. Collateral damage, that is civilian deaths and private property damage, increased as a result.

Much more ominous was a development that started on August 26th. One German bomber accidentally released a few bombs onto London proper, and caused only small damage. Churchill was worried that Hitler might be relenting on his promise not to bomb London, and ordered his own bombers to attack Berlin over the next few nights. Hitler, in turn, saw this as evidence of Churchill reneging, and declared his intention to bomb London as soon as the logistics could be organised. When this happened, September 6th, it marked the end of Phase Two of the Battle, and the beginning of the deadly Phase Three.

A DELAYED RESPONSE ON SHEEPSKINS

Letters, Selwyn King, Hon. Treasurer, CWA Sheep Skin Vest Committee. Your correspondent, "Commissioner," says sheep skin vests supplied in the last war were absolute failures. While their value for the infantry was limited, for the reasons stated by your correspondent, and also because the infantry were not able to carry the vests in addition to their packs, they were, nevertheless, of great benefit to the transport, the Navy and Air Force.

The writer spent three winters in France during the last war, and can state definitely that large numbers of vests were used and very much appreciated by the men engaged in transport work, day and night exposed to the bitter cold of the winters in France. The same remarks apply to the Navy, and also to both the ground staff and airmen of the Australian flying squadrons.

Conditions are very different in this war. A large proportion of the army is now mechanised, and there will be vastly greater numbers of men on transport work who will be grateful for the sheep skin vests. The Air Force and the Navy (all of whom were consulted before any move was made to prepare the vests) are anxiously awaiting supplies.

Fifty vests have been handed over to the Navy for use by men on the mine-sweepers, and 100 vests have been handed over to the RAAF for d1spatch to our men who are manning the Sunderland flying-boats in Iceland.

We hope to be able to keep up a continuous supply in answer to the requests from the three sections of our fighting forces abovementioned, who have already stated that more than 10,000 vests are required for men in the colder climates, and this number will probably increase as the war proceeds and therefore our appeal for support to the movement, which has approval of the Australian Comforts Fund.

GOVERNMENT PASSES WAR BILL

Menzies and his government were working in their own way to improve the nation's readiness. On July 22, the Parliament passed the National Security Act. This was an Act that "permits the Government to make regulations requiring persons to place themselves and their property at the disposal of the Commonwealth to secure public safety, the defence of the Commonwealth and territories, and the efficient prosecution of the War."

Comment. This was an Act that gave the Government unlimited and undefined powers to do what it liked to anyone and anything. It opened the way to the most dreadful and arbitrary course of action, unfettered by any reference to citizens' rights. The repercussions were potentially as severe as any that the totalitarian States had reserved for themselves, yet it passed almost unremarked. The *SMH* noted it as a half-column on Page 15, and there was no editorial or correspondence on it.

This was because the Australian people trusted the Government not to use the Act in a draconian way. As we have seen, there were plenty of folk who were ready to criticise both sides of politics, but, in the long run, no one thought that the Act would be abused in practice. And that trust was well placed, as it turned out. Though, next month, as we will see, the newspapers had cause to doubt the accuracy of that statement.

GERMAN PROPAGANDA, LORD HAW HAW

William Joyce was born in 1906 in America of English parents. He spent his teens in Ireland, and in the early 1930s became prominent in the many Fascist Parties then flourishing in London. As war approached he moved to Germany, and got a job in the Ministry of Propaganda as an English-speaking foreign language broadcaster. He held that position from September 1939 until he went into hiding at the end of April, 1945. He was executed in England in January, 1946 as a traitor.

His evening 20-minute broadcasts were widely listened to, especially during 1939 and 1940. The BBC estimated that in that period he had a British audience of six millions adults who listened every day or every second day, and another 18 million occasional auditors. He was awarded the honorific title of Lord Haw Haw by his appreciative audience.

Why did they listen? It seems that one important reason is that German reports were right up to date, whereas the BBC and official military reports were often days behind. People knew that things were going on, and they reckoned that if they were being starved of information by the British, then they were better off getting some idea from the admittedly biased reports offered by the Germans. Then in a day's time, they could put that all together with the equally biased reports from Britain, and perhaps get some sort of realistic picture. As time went on, more and more listeners tuned in to scoff; his initial message was losing its effectiveness for them, because it was too clearly propaganda laid on with a heavy hand. But others – probably a small minority after a while – listened from fear that all he said was true.

HAW HAW'S WORDS OF WISDOM

A typical outburst:

> Your Winston is talking a lot these days about putting a blockade round us. Perhaps you could explain to him that Germany now has the natural resources of France, Belgium, Holland, Luxemburg, Norway, Poland, Czechoslovakia, and Austria, Russia, and of course Germany, at her disposal. He can put his ships anywhere he likes, and we will not notice them. Unless they get in our way when we start to export our surpluses to the rest of the world. Tell him that his blockade is as silly as he is.
>
> Our invasion of Britain is certainly coming soon, but what I want to impress upon you is

that nothing you can do is really of the slightest use. Don't be deceived by this lull before the storm, because, although there is still the chance of peace, Hitler is aware of the political and economic confusion in England, and is only waiting for the right moment. Then, when his moment comes, he will strike, and strike hard.

It will not be long before Britain has to yield to the invincible might of German arms, for Germany started when the war began, and was equipped before that. But this also I feel, that short as the time may be, every day will have the length of a year for the people whom Churchill has condemned to ruin in his crazy and fantastic plan to blockade Europe.

BAD TIMES AHEAD IN UK

NEWS ITEM. In July, 258 British civilians were killed by the enemy and 321 seriously injured. Since then the air attacks have been greatly intensified, and, although the enemy has achieved only meagre military results, it is already evident that the civilian casualties this month will be considerably higher than those in July.

OZ NEWS, VIEWS AND TRIVIA

Bob Menzies was fed up. He had tried to get an extension of Parliament so he could stay there indefinitely, and everyone was against this. So he took another tack. He decided to call an early election, in September instead of December, to hopefully get an extension for three years. He reasoned, correctly, that he had never been chosen by the people as Prime Minister. He had just inherited that position after Joseph Lyons died. He had been sitting on an uneasy alliance of two parties, the United Party and the Country Party, with lots of dissident members in each.

Also, his reign had started in peace, but was now in an all-consuming war. He and his Government were under constant criticism for the way they were doing things. Could he gain re-election as a war-time Prime Minister, and could he get a broad mandate from the people to prosecute the war as he wished? There was one way to find out, and that was to ask the people to vote on it. So, on August 21st, **he announced a Federal election to be held one month hence, on September 21st.**

NO SYDNEY EASTER SHOW IN 1941

Sir Samual Hordern had announced that the Royal Easter Show would not be held next year. The Army had taken over the Ground, and could not release it. Sir Samual had consulted with the Prime Minister on this matter, and they had made the decision jointly. He regretted the necessity of closing the Show, and realised that much of value would be lost as a consequence. But he considered that the benefits derived by the Army were greater, and hence his decision.

Various members of the public spoke up in support of the decision. The Pure Bred Cattle Breeders Association said that every Member would applaud the decision, although they all deplored its necessity. The President of the Graziers Association of NSW, who was also an officer of the United Stud Beef Cattle Breeders Association said that it was sufficient that the Showground was to be needed by the soldiers, and that must be the end of it.

Others were not quite so malleable. The Lord Mayor of Sydney considered that a blunder had been made. "There is ample time for the military to find other accommodation." The Manager of the Bank of NSW opined that it was a very grave mistake, and that all of rural NSW had an interest in the running of the Show. The Lord Mayor of Brisbane triumphantly reported that the Brisbane Show would certainly be held, and the Governor of Queensland applauded the decision.

Letters, H McWilliam. The loss to the business community will be far in excess of the 300,000 Pounds which authorities state would be the cost of providing a suitable alternate camp site.

Easter fortnight is looked upon as the period when business losses are made good. Without the Show, many people who are already feeling the effect of war-time saving resulting in a general curtailment of business will find it impossible to carry on or else, in the case of more substantial firms, they will be compelled to reduce staff.

By and large the cancellation of the Show will cause immense loss of business, and create unemployment.

Letters, A Alanson. Can I suggest another reason why the Show should be held? It is the maintenance of morale throughout the whole community. When a ship is storm-stricken, when a fire is consuming premises and endangering lives the panic likely to result is prevented by those who go steadily about their jobs. Throughout Australia today the pain-inflicting throbs of war are intensely felt, and every effort is being made to help, but the foundations of success rest upon the strong, quiet sense of carrying on with concerns of everyday life.

The disruptions of business caused by the war are being met every day by calm adjustment. This steadfast maintenance of our confidence is absolutely necessary. Going on with the affairs of everyday life expresses and preserves our confidence. The spirit is the thing. We fight, we work, we keep on our way.

Letters, D Cargill. The show is the mainstay of the marketing for the breeders who have done so much to improve the livestock in this country. Then there is the ordinary farmer or grazier who wishes to improve his stock: he trusts to this show for guidance as to the class and strain he should purchase. The information and education he receives during judging of the many classes is of great importance. This also applies to the fodder classes in which there is a wealth of information.

Letters, Frederick Aarons, Ex-servicemen's War Emergency Association, Sydney. There is in the community a most dangerous attitude of mind embodied in the paradoxical slogan "Business as usual," a contention that this country can play a full part in the colossal struggle for existence against a merciless and powerful foe, and still continue to live a normal peacetime life. It must be clearly understood that this is a total war, and can only be won by total measures. We need the total effort of the nation prepared to drop every material advantage to take up every sacrifice in the common fight.

For these reasons, our Association believes that in the **present circumstances the holding of the Royal Show would not be in the best interests of the nation at war.**

Letters, H Sivyer. If the brains, energy, and money used by exhibitors at the Sydney Show were utilised in defence precautions, such as a balloon barrage and air-raid shelters, the result would pay better dividends than the Show, which, if held, will bring another 50,000 potential air-raid victims to a city which lends itself to air attack.

One high-explosive bomb on the arch of the Harbour Bridge might do more damage to Sydney's business than any postponement of the Show.

Letter, A Comonsoli, Greta Camp. No wonder the Army wants to stay at the Show Ground. It is close to shops, the beaches, the race tracks, the pubs and night clubs, the city, and all the best things of city living. They have none of the tough conditions that they would find in real Army camps. If anyone needs field exercises, they will have to be trucked miles and miles away to get them. And of course it will be of no use to any one who has to go off and fight overseas, but we will need fat sleek Officers and NCO's, so we might as well pool them in the one spot.

Comment. This Letter must have **just** sneaked through censorship.

BRITISH CHILDREN FOR AUSTRALIA

News item. Some British parents wished to see their children removed completely from a land that was subject to capricious bombing at random times. One solution was to fall in with the various forms of on-and-off migration schemes to the country, but another was to send them to good families overseas.

The first batch of these children is on its way to Melbourne and Sydney. In total, in this first batch there are 251 boys and 228 girls. These will go mainly to NSW and Victoria, because the ship visits only the two ports there. In later batches, the other States will have this ratio corrected.

Only 16 of these children have been allocated to specific sponsors, and the remainder will be allocated by State authorities by the time the ship has arrived. It is expected that 330 of the children will be sent to sponsors nominated by the parents, but this will be subject to confirmation by State authorities. The rest will be allocated to 3,000 relatives and friends who have registered their names with authorities as prospective guardians.

INTERNMENT OF REFUGEES

The debate on this topic continued, but most of the opinions published were much the same as earlier. The view expressed below is sufficiently different to warrant its inclusion here.

Letters, E Johnston. Experience has shown that in Norway, Holland, Belgium, and France, no country which is at war with or even threatened by Germany and Italy can afford to neglect any precautions against the "enemy within." The difficulty is that most of the aliens in Australia came here as refugees, and while one naturally desires that they receive consideration, they all must understand that we are at war, and that as a consequence they must and should suffer willingly such inconvenience as may be considered necessary in the interest of public safety.

Love of country is the first thing that is instilled into a man from birth; therefore, we should be doubly careful even of the naturalised alien. Country of birth will always come first. **Internment should not be regarded as a penalty but as a sacrifice towards victory.** If these foreigners are so anxious to confirm our faith in their loyalty to Britain's cause, they should stop complaining and make work easier for all of us to win the war.

SEPTEMBER: THE BLITZ OF LONDON

The first week in September was pretty bad. The Germans kept up their raids on airfields and strategic targets and as well dropped an increasing load on civilian targets, outside of London. Their aim in this latter venture was to give the idea that no one was safe and to spread panic, and then capitulation, through the population. The trouble for the Nazis was that the more the Brits were bombed, the more resolute they got.

The other German problem was that the RAF continued to knock their planes, and aircrews, out of the sky at twice the rate that they themselves were suffering. It was all adding up, and at the same time Britain's production of everything was still on the increase. Hitler might have expected that his strategic bombing would take a big toll on production, but this was not the case. What was the point in doing this any more?

So, when September 8th came, and he ordered his revenge attacks on London, it made sense that he should abandon his strategic bombing, and **turn to terror tactics**. His aim now was **to destroy the morale of London**, the stronghold of the nation, and to make it realise that he could use his weapons of destruction to force it into subjugation. So for the next 10 days, he implemented his **third Phase of the Battle**, the indiscriminate bombing of the civilian population of London.

During this Phase, every day and night, sirens would sound, and most people would move to the shelters that had been waiting for almost two years. They might stay there a couple of hours, then go back to their activities, and then respond a few hours later to another siren call. This just kept on happening, as much in the night as in the day. Some of them would be killed, some injured, some would have their house destroyed, it was just a deadly gamble that they were caught up in. The Blitz had come, at last, and the Brits were proving their mettle.

Mind you, it was not all one-way traffic. The RAF was still making big raids on German cities, and even giving Mussolini's northern cities a work-out. By now, the policy of not attacking enemy cities was wearing a bit thin, but more often that not, the targets were still industrial, and military bases and aerodromes. But the British raids were becoming increasingly effective, and further, the German population was itself getting the idea that perhaps Britain would not be a pushover as promised. Maybe Hitler had got something wrong, for a change.

The Phase Three bombings kept up until September 17th. On that day, England enjoyed its largest air victory ever, claiming that 185 enemy aircraft were shot down. A total of 131 bombers were included in this haul, and only 25 British machines were lost. This huge loss for Germany came only after the loss of 181 planes two days earlier, and the air battle was becoming a rout.

Hitler faced reality. His invasion fleet had been blasted to ribbons by the RAF bombing, and the Channel weather was becoming violent as winter approached. His large fleet of barges, now much reduced, idling in French ports, would be lucky to make the distance across the Channel. His air offensive, to destroy British facilities and to break the spirit of the nation, had failed badly. In fact, the nation was more resolute that ever before. And further, he had lost over 1600 planes and almost as many trained airmen in his processes.

He quietly announced that **Sea Lion was postponed indefinitely. The invasion of Britain was off for a year**, and as it turned out, it was off forever.

Churchill, and his Chiefs of Staff, intercepted Hitler's announcement and, being pretty sure it was genuine, suggested that they leave their bunker and "we should all take a little fresh air." The news percolated through society over the next few weeks and, as it was appreciated, was a glorious blessing to a relieved nation that wholeheartedly gave its thanks to God and the RAF.

The bombing of London did not stop. It kept up at about half the ferocity until the end of October, then went quieter for the Winter months. In Spring, full-scale raids started again, though again at half-ferocity, and lasted until May 10th, 1941. Over the eight months of the Blitz, 43,000 Londoners were killed, and over a million houses destroyed. At one stage, raids occurred for 76 consecutive nights.

WHAT'S HAPPENING IN FRANCE?

The French were still blinking at the light. The North was occupied on a military basis. The South was "Free", and occupied by consent. That is, the Government, now living in the small city of Vichy, was ruling with the consent of the Germans. **It had declared itself neutral for the purposes of the War.** Marshall Petain, was the "Head of State", and was trying to stave off growing German pressure to join the fray. In the meantime, the German authorities who were running the country, had arrested the leading politicians from six months ago and charged them with ignoring Hitler's various pleas for peace, and thereby precipitating the War with Germany. These included Daladier, and Reynaud, the top two men in the nation. In effect, if found guilty, they would be declared war criminals.

The trial was being held in camera, starting at the end of September, and the verdict was expected during the next few months. A number of commentators in the British press pointed out that if Hitler was to successfully invade Britain, it would be most likely that **Churchill, Chamberlain and their Cabinets would face a similar fate.**

When the French capitulated, half of its overseas French Empire accepted that, and the other half opted for supporting Free France, led in exile from London by Charles de Gaulle. This General, at the end of September, led a foray into the West African city of Dakar, which was remaining loyal to Vichy. He expected the citizens there would rise up, and declare themselves loyal to the Free French. He barged into Dakar with a flotilla, including the Oz cruiser Australia, flexed his military muscles with plenty of support from the Brits, and got egg all over his face. A few days later he, and the Government, were roundly criticised in Parliament for the fiasco, but the thing that was learned was that this French colony at least was quite content to go under German subjugation, and probably gain more control over its own destiny than it had previously experienced. Over the next few weeks, it turned out that a number of other French colonies thought the same.

Indo China was a nation bordering on the South of China. It remained loyal to the Free French. But it no longer had the military backing of that former nation. In this period of weakness, the Japanese, fighting flat-out to conquer China, saw an opportunity. They insisted that Indo China open up its railways to carry its troops to the border, and that it should in effect clear its borders so that the Japanese could attack China from the South. The Free French were reluctant to do this, and at the end of September there was something of a stalemate.

But the Japanese did eventually gain large footholds in Indo China, and these would become important just over a year later when Japan's military might sought to invade Singapore and Australia.

THE OZ FEDERAL ELECTION.

Federal elections were scheduled for September 21st. Menzies had called them in something of a hurry, so he needed to tidy up a few things that might cost him votes.

First, it should be remembered that, only a few weeks ago, he was advocating that Parliament should not face an election at all. Instead, he wanted it to go on to some indefinite date, after the War. So, at this point there was not much he could do to explain his sudden change of heart, and the best he could say was that things changed so quickly.

Second, his Government had been dithering for months over the introduction of petrol rationing. They started with a set of proposals that were quite silly, and gradually modified them down to a reasonable set of rules. And then they announced that they would be introduced in early September. Bob Menzies now took an interest. Surely, such an unpopular move could not start just before an election. Surely, voter resentment would be too high, and many people would vote against the Government. No, this must be avoided at all cost! So, in a fiendishly cunning move, he decided to bring in petrol rationing on the Saturday after the election, and by then the poor dumb public would have forgotten their resentment. Who said politicians aren't on the ball!!

Third, all his plans, to introduce restrictions and censorship for the Press and radio, were scrubbed. He decided that his Propaganda Department would force access only if the Press actually published something and he needed to make a correction. In that case, the Press would be forced to carry the Government's statement of the true position as it saw it. This was about as far away from the position, as originally proposed, as you could get, and it represented a major back-down. A cynic might suggest that the change in policy was occasioned by the upcoming election, and by Menzies' fear of going into that with a hostile Press. Surely not!!

Fourth, Mr Menzies announced that, after consideration, **the Sydney Show would be held next year at the Showground after all**, and that the Military would vacate the ground for the duration. Once again the cynic might have something to say, but I remind him that this is War-time, and such thoughts are not at all patriotic. Please desist!!

ELECTION ISSUES

The essential argument was over the conduct of the War. Menzies wanted approval to continue with his current policies, while John Curtin, representing Labor, wanted to apply the brakes. In a particular point of difference, he wanted our Servicemen to be kept here to defend our shores, while Menzies was glad to show his loyalty to the Home Country by sending any men he could recruit as soon as they were ready. Another issue was their attitudes to conscription.

Could men be called up for the Military, and then after training, be forced to serve overseas, in spheres such as Europe and Africa? Menzies said that they should. Curtin and Labor were much more careful, and the most they would admit to was that perhaps some few might be sent into the Pacific region or perhaps the big British base in Singapore. This was a major difference between the Parties, and was one that would come back to bedevil them for the next few years.

In the run-up to the elections, Curtin weakened his case by promising a number of financial benefits for voters, such as old-age pensioners. Everyone knew we were not in a position to give any hand-outs, and he was lambasted constantly for this. Menzies campaigned on his record, admitting his Government had made some mistakes, and pleaded that the great rush to War had made decision-making difficult and uncertain.

The Press, no longer worried about proposals for censorship, weighed in behind Menzies with all their might. The *SMH* published about thirty Letters supporting Menzies, and **one only supporting Labor and Curtin**. Likewise, campaign funding for newspapers advertisements was one-sided. The United Party had multiple large ads in every edition, and Labor could muster only one or two ads of about 8-column-inches. Menzies also stole a march by linking his ads with images of Churchill, and the valiant people and Military of Britain.

LETTERS ON THE ELECTION

There was a wide choice of glowing testimonials for Menzies and the United Party. I have included just three of these, and the only one for the Labor Party that the *SMH* published. All of these, and the others, are quite emotional, and that is a sign of the times. I add a final Letter, which if it did not admire Menzies' ethics, did admire his political cunning.

Letters, T Ryan. The British people are valiantly and uncomplainingly meeting the grim sacrifices to which the German war on Great Britain is subjecting them. Loss of homes, prolonged mental and physical suffering, mangled bodies, and death are their sacrificial contributions to the war. And because this war is being fought by Great Britain to protect the British Empire, and therefore Australia, from domination by a merciless foe, the sacrifices of the British people are vicarious in character. Are they not being borne for us here in Australia, since the British people are meeting and resisting an invasion which will determine our destiny as a free and democratic people?

Do we not, then, owe to Great Britain some measure of reciprocal sacrifice? Let them who deny it stand out and declare themselves but at the same time hang their heads in shame. Let all others respond to the Prime Minister's appeal to all good Australians to offer some contribution to our war effort in the form of unremitting work and sacrifice, financial and personal, and show their sincerity by helping to return Mr Menzies to power on Saturday.

By doing so, we shall show that in some measure we share with our brave fellow British kinsmen and kinswomen that sacrificial spirit which they have so magnificently displayed. To put something into the Commonwealth Treasury, not to take something out, is one of our tasks in our war effort, and one form of sacrifice.

Letters, J Trumble. I suggest that electors in the coming election desirous of doing their best to help to win the war in which the Empire is now fighting alone for its very existence would do well to eliminate from consideration side issues and personal feeling, and give consideration only to the question as to which of the opposing parties should, in the best interests of the cause, be chosen to carry on our war effort in the grave situation in which we are now placed. In the first year of the war when there should have been unity there has been political disunion involving misrepresentation and unjust criticism of the work done in our war effort.

In the Prime Minister we have a leader who is looked upon in the mother Country as Australia's present-day outstanding public man. Of great ability, he has worked hard and given of his best, often in very trying circumstances. It might be well to here draw attention to a statement made by our great Empire leader, Winston Churchill, on the occasion of his memorable broadcast upon the French surrender in June last. Mr Churchill said, inter alia, "What has happened in France makes no difference in British faith and purpose. We have become the sole champions now in arms to defend the world cause – we shall do our best to be worthy of that high honour."

In this election we have the war records of the parties for guidance, and on this it can be said the Government has done all that could reasonably be required of it, whereas the Labor

Party has not. To use a sporting term, the Labor Party has not pulled its weight.

Letters, M Bass. Surely our women folk will not be led away by hollow speeches, and if we women only wake up now, even at the eleventh hour, we may save the situation, and perhaps, the world from tragic disaster, and so atone a little for our shortcomings in the past. I feel strongly that we have sadly neglected the opportunities given us when the vote was extended to all adults. I often think what we might have done with it, and wonder why we have done so little. Instead of throwing our weight in where it would have had the best effect, we have been content to use our emancipation to share fully the pleasures of the world.

I ask women of the Labor Party, UCP and UAP to throw their whole strength in the common lot, and vote for the men who are truly loyal to the British Empire, and so, loyal to us, those who have proved it in their lives past, not by a sudden somersault on eve of election. Let us throw aside party creed, or self interest as Britain has done. Any compromise today is unthinkable, and leaves loopholes for the Fifth Column, which never sleeps. Vote in a body for the other column, the column led by Mr Churchill, which Mr Menzies is trying so hard to lead in Australia. Help him in this endeavour, even though he may not have so far done all we could wish, remember he is bound by human limitations as we all are, and anyway what have we women as a whole done to help him?

Letters, John Wood. Please allow me to correct the impression which might easily be gained from a perusal of your correspondence columns, that all your readers are supporters of the present Federal Government.

I feel sure that all will agree that the crying need at the present time is for national unity. Such unity can only be a reality if the great mass of the Australian people is able to have complete faith in the sincerity of its Government. What thinking person can consider the record of the present Federal government and still have faith in its sincerity?

Mr Menzies says that he is deeply concerned with the preservation of individual liberty – and orders the police to search the homes of Australian citizens and seize their belongings. He says that he is in favour of freedom of thought and speech – and suppresses working-class publications and attempts to muzzle the remainder of the Press. Mr Menzies asks the people to follow the Government along the path of just and equal sacrifice – and, after a year of war, companies still pay dividends of 10 to 15 percent, after making liberal provision for the Government's wartime taxation. It is not the Labor leaders, but Mr Menzies and his followers, who are the real saboteurs of national unity.

As a firm believer in the need for real national unity, as distinct from the sham variety sponsored by Mr Menzies and Cameron, I propose to vote Labor on September 21.

Letters, C Robinson. In conclusion, let me congratulate Mr Menzies for his choice of election date. There is no better time to rally people to the flag than when they under attack from an enemy. Mr Menzies has skilfully used that fact by realising that England, and hence ourselves, is under the greatest possible attack of all times, and that will stir the patriotism in every man's heart. My Labor friends at the pub say this is exploiting our noble sentiments. I disagree. It is his job to win the election, and if this helps him to win, then I commend him for doing so.

ELECTION RESULTS

The elections were duly held on September 21st. The result: nothing changed. A few people lost their seats, a few gained. No one of any importance came or went. Every thing stayed much the same. The only result of significance was that Menzies could now say that, unlike before, he was elected by the people, and that they had given him a mandate to continue with his policies. But he was still to be plagued by the fact that he had to share power with the Country Party, and by the fact that John Curtin would not join him in a National Government that bucked the two-party system on War issues. It was these two issues, and conscription, that proved his undoing next year.

OCTOBER: HITLER LOOKS ELSEWHERE

I would like to jump to the end of this month. By then, it was clear that the intensity of bombing in the nation, and in London, had dropped off. Granted, the damage was still terrible, and the number of deaths and injuries was almost beyond comprehension, but Herr Hitler was obviously sending fewer bombers to visit, and it was now obvious to all that he no longer dreamed of invasion.

At the same time, however, the bombing of enemy targets by the British was reaching new heights. Germany and Italy, were the lucky recipients of the free aerial presents delivered nightly by the RAF. It was said officially in Britain that strategic targets only were attacked, and that may have been so. But it was quite clear that civilians were also sometimes getting in the way, and the devastation shown daily in the German papers was definitely not all faked. Argument was raging at Home about whether policy should change. That is, should the RAF go forth and deliberately bomb enemy civilians? After all, many Londoners argued, the Germans are trying to kill us. Why should we not return the compliment? Are we just sitting ducks?

Surely if they got the same medicine they would call off their bombings, in the expectation that we would then do the same. Churchill and his War Cabinet saw the issue in more strategic terms. They argued that the task of the RAF was to destroy the enemy's factories and airfields and bridges and so on. That is, to damage permanently their capacity to continue the War. In any case they argued, the bombing of London had not weakened the will of the British to fight on. Why would we expect that our bombings of their cities would be any more effective?

Arguments came thick and fast. They ranged from simply wanting to get revenge and destroy the entire German race, to those that preached creeds of love they neighbour. One extreme example of this latter argument came from Percival Travers of Oxford who wrote that we "should suspend all military operations for two days, even our defence of London and the Channel, and have two days of non-stop prayer for an immediate peace. We could inform the German people we intended to do this, and it is highly likely that they would reciprocate. Surely this is better than the current slaughter we have, in defiance of God's wishes."

One correspondent saw it quite differently again.

Letters, J Courtauld. The life of the human family can not prosper if it is to be governed by logical considerations alone and common sense is of no value unless tempered by sentiment. If German barbarities succeed in winning this war the cause of civilization will receive a mortal blow. If they are defeated by like barbarities the result will be little better.

But if, as I am convinced can be done, they are defeated by those who have striven to preserve such decencies and humanities as past generations have gradually introduced into the hideous business of slaughter, history will tell our descendants that even war could not force mankind to a backward step. Surely this is what we are fighting for? I will not attempt to define a moral or immoral act, but perhaps the man who ordered our soldiers, sailors, or airmen deliberately to attack the poor, the weak, and the defenceless would not be left with a clear conscience.

It is distressing and ominous to find that intelligent and clear-thinking people can make such a good case for our abandonment of rules of conduct to which we have always adhered, and it seems to indicate that Herr Hitler's theories are making headway even in this country.

In any case, for the time being, official policy remained that civilian areas should not be bombed. In practice, there were many occasions when the bombs strayed. As time went on, this policy was relaxed to the point that, towards the end of the War, German cities were deliberately targeted and bombed to smithereens. Then, going forward just a few years, the US went to the ultimate when it atom-bombed the Japanese cities of Nagasaki and Hiroshima.

WHAT HITLER DID NEXT

For all of October, the RAF continued to bomb the "invasion ports" on the coast of France, just to make sure Hitler did not change his mind about invading Britain. But, no, he did not, and he turned instead towards the other jolly plans he had for bringing joy to the world. Towards the end of October, he tried to enlist the aid of General Franco, the newly ensconced dictator of Spain, in a move that would expel the British from their bases in Gibraltar.

This Rock, on the bottom of Spain, was a large island that commanded the entrance to the Mediterranean, and was vital for access to the Balkans, Italy, Greece, Turkey, North Africa and the Suez Canal. In other words, it was quite important to all the trade and supplies that Britain cherished and Hitler coveted. So, Hitler got in his

10-carriage train and went to the border of Spain to con Franco into joining the war against the Brits.

Franco, looking as usual "like a small-town barber of Seville", had just had a civil war on his hands for almost three years, and he knew his country was exhausted. So, he sort-of promised Hitler that he **might** join his crusade at **some indefinite time** in the future, after Hitler had given him enormous supplies of everything. Hitler, and his Foreign Minister Ribbentrop blustered as usual, but Franco remained as bland as could be, and maintained his promises for the future. This was Hitler's first **disappointment of October.**

Thoroughly frustrated, Hitler took a train ride back to Paris. Here, he had his **second disappointment**. What he wanted was to conclude a formal Peace Treaty with the Vichy French, in which they surrendered lots of Empire and gave up a ton of national assets. Marshall Petain, aged 85 years and getting older every day, over a period of a few days remained formal, aloof and undaunted, and again played for time. Hitler left Paris for Italy in a bad mood, not happy.

When he got there, right at the end of the month, he was informed by Mussolini that Italy had just invaded Greece. Benito poured forth all the usual excuses for invasions, about Italians in Greece being given a hard time, but what he really said was that he invaded because he wanted to and he could. He wanted the military glory he felt came with conquests, and he wanted the spoils of war that victories brought. Hitler hit the angry button again, but he gritted his teeth and acted quite civilly to Il Duce. But the Italian move opened up a whole can of worms, with huge consequences in the Balkans, and we will come back to these in the next Chapters. Just to finish off here, I add with some small glee, that this was **Hitler's third disappointment for October**. Really, despite his long run of good months prior to this, it had been a bad month for him. Was it a harbinger of things to come?

MEANWHILE, BACK IN BRITAIN …..

Life in Britain was still going on, but not at all as normal. To show just the smallest bit of this, I have included three items from *The Times*.

> **First item, H Talbot.** It was market day, and the famous old town was all activity as is customary on such occasions. About the luncheon hour the familiar notes of the warning siren sounded. Acting on the Prime Minister's request, **business for the greater part proceeded as usual**. Farmers, salesmen, drivers, shopkeepers all carried on in defiance of the worst Germany could do, and it was good to watch, and one felt proud of the spirit displayed by the inhabitants of the county town, its adjacent villages and hamlets – but alas there was one prominent exception.
>
> My errand took me to the Sessions House, home of most official Departments of the county. I arrived by appointment at 3pm to find the doors closed and the numerous staff, servants of the public, safely ensconced in their air-raid shelters beneath the steel and concrete many storeyed building. Some 40 or 50 of the said public were waiting in the street, all anxious to get their business in the building completed; the remarks and comments of these citizens were bitter and condemning in the extreme, and would hardly

have been mitigated had they known, what I subsequently learnt, that the closure was by order of the Minister of Home Security.

At this stage of the proceedings a wedding coach passed by, complete with its white streamers, presumably to play its part in the wedding ceremony, evidently the happy couple were not to be deterred – good fortune to them.

Surely the nation is being badly served by the Cabinet Minister who, when the public generally and gallant personnel of all Services are carrying on their duties uninterruptedly, forces a public Department, against the wishes of the employees therein to dance so faithfully to the tune Hitler calls.

Second News item. It is now an offence to sell cream, and the cream-jug must disappear from the table of all law-abiding citizens. The Ministry of Food has estimated that the prohibition of the sale of cream will, in a normal year, release 70,000,000 gallons of milk for other purposes. While the nation is not likely to go short of liquid milk even in the dead of winter, it is well to keep on the safe side and to make certain that there is a margin of safety to meet all demands. For one reason or another the rate of milk consumption has increased in many districts. In times of stress and hurry milk is a sustaining and easily digested food. Then there is the National Milk Scheme, under which the younger generation are taking more milk at a reduced price. From every point of view it is desirable to assure an ample supply of milk for all who want it, and the prohibition of the sale of cream will help to do this, and will also free additional milk for the manufacture of more essential dairy products such as cheese in the summer.

The Ministry of Food regards cream as a luxury in war-time, which it is, but it is worth recalling the by-product of cream manufacture, separated milk, was not wasted even in days of embarrassing plenty. Much of it was tinned as condensed milk. Then scald milk, the by-product of clotted cream has always been appreciated in the West Country and its food value was far from negligible. The fat removed in the cream could be made good by butter or margarine, and the family which had plenty of separated milk or scald milk bought at a low price was not ill-nourished. The National Milk Scheme, however, should remove any cause of hardship in these cases, and the absence of cream from the tables of the better-to-do cannot be counted a serious sacrifice if it ensures an ample supply of milk for all sections of the community.

Third news item. The form of challenge to be made by sentries, and the correct answer, are set out in Air Ministry Orders.

Any person approaching is to be challenged: "Halt, who goes there?" On receiving the answer "Friend," the sentry is to respond, "Advance one to be recognized." ("One" means one person.) If the party challenged consists of more than one person the challenge is to be repeated for each.

If a person challenged does not halt, he is to be challenged in this manner: "Halt, or I fire." If he does not then halt, he is to be challenged once more in this manner, but if he still does not halt and no means are available to stop him, the sentry is instructed to fire, aiming low to hit but not to kill.

Where a person who has been challenged can be stopped by some other means – such as by calling on the guard – the sentry is not to shoot.

DID AN OZ ELECTION JUST HAPPEN?

The Federal election had come and gone. When the dust settled a month later, people were scratching their heads and asking if it had made any difference. In the new Government, Menzies and his UAP still held power, and Labor was still in Opposition. The UAP, and its coalition partner the Country Party, together still had a narrow majority in the House of Reps, and it was now down to only a few seats. So the Government felt insecure, but at the same time, Labor was waiting for an opportunity to pounce.

Menzies, after the election, was keen on forming a National Government. This meant that all parties would come together on matters related to the War and form agreed National war-time policies. It also meant that because all parties had agreed to those policies, no one could be singled out for criticism for any part of it. And this in turn effectively meant that the Government could not be turned out of office.

On the other side of the fence, Labor and Curtin could see that the Coalition was only loosely held together, and that Labor might well be able to oust it. Why would they deprive themselves of that chance, when they felt that they could do a better job any way?

So, despite the good and indeed noble intentions of many politicians, and various attempts over the course of the month to get together a National Government, no such Government was formed. Many people had their say on this.

Letters, W Page. It is inconceivable to me that differences of opinion should exist among those who are governing this country during a time of war. The voices of 7,000,000 people cry for leadership. We have given these men the honour of guiding us in a time of crisis. The least they can do in return is to try and forget any petty differences and as true Australians work in harmony.

Today we face the greatest trial of any nation: its ability to stand on its own feet and proudly and firmly carry the banner of Democracy. Other nations have perished through lack of foresight on the part of their leaders, petty differences, and selfishness. That our war effort should be impeded is part of the Nazi scheme, and disunity in our midst will impede it. Those who call themselves Australians must act as Australians, and, like our fighting men, be prepared to give their best.

Letters, F B. The results of the recent elections surely showed that Australia has no wish for party government at the present time, but it appears that our elected representatives have failed to realise the feeling of the electors.

The existence of political parties is the root cause of the deadlock. Loyalty to party seems to be regarded by the politicians as of more importance than the vital needs of the country.

Would that we had some power that would enable us to place all parties in cold storage for the duration of the war! Lock, stock, and barrel, all party organisations and associations, offices and branches, funds and property, caucuses and committees – put them all into the freezer until Hitlerism is cold. Forbid the contribution of funds to any party – and also the collection of money or kind for party purposes. Close up the party rooms at Parliament House, and let the whole of the members in collective conclave deliberate and decide upon the measures to be taken by a united people for our preservation.

Then there would be some chance of a leader of the nation arising – not a leader of a Party, for there would be no such thing for the time being. Perhaps, too, it may result in party politics disappearing for a generation.

Letters, C Hardwick, Phillip Street, Sydney. One asks then, what can the people of Australia do? I suggest this is the answer. Let every Mayor or head of every local government body throughout this great continent convene a public meeting of the men and women of their districts to meet together on the same date, at the same time and voice a public protest against our politics which will compel them to appreciate realities and the demands of the people.

I venture the opinion that the people will say to all political parties "We want you to remember we as a people are fighting for our very existence, for all those things we cherish, for freedom, for truth, and for justice. We want you to forget there are any political parties. We want a Government formed of the best offering, men who will realise what Australia means to the Empire, particularly in the Pacific." No time can be lost, no time should be lost. Only by prompt nation-wide action do I see the possibility of a National Government.

WHAT IS CONTEMPORARY ART?

I was brought up in a small coal-mining village of 2,000 poverty-stricken people, living in death's shadow. Half them were Geordies from the Old Country, and the rest were locals with education to the age of 13, if lucky. Not surprisingly, there was not a great deal of discussion about art. If anyone ever thought about it, they saw portraits, landscapes, and cottage scenes, perhaps a bit idealised, but certainly true to life.

But, this version of the art world, common round much of Australia, was being shattered by the new, revolutionary world of contemporary art. Or it might be called abstract art, or modern art, at different times. In any case, it was all the same. It showed ridiculous images of disembodied eyes, floating in air, of cars on giraffes' legs, and of queerly shaped houses not touching earth. To miners, and working class folk, it was complete and utter rubbish.

But in more sophisticated Sydney and Melbourne, it was more or less in vogue in some quarters. Small galleries were touting it and now, in these cities, large exhibitions were being held by the Contemporary Arts Society. In Melbourne, paintings of the Old Masters were being placed in storage to make way for these new masterpieces in the Victorian Art Gallery.

Not everyone liked what was going on.

Letters, Novem. Champions of contemporary art would gain more consideration if they would set out in definite terms the aims of the movement. Hitherto their claims to recognition seem to be base largely on a negation of the established order. If they would have liberty, let them frame their charter.

While asking for enlightenment as to just what the innovators are seeking to bring about, might one suggest, also, that they should be just a trifle less esoteric in their language. Imagine, for example, an ordinary mortal trying to discover the meaning of "Neo-organic Figuration!"

Letters, An Unbeliever. One must pity the subconscious mind of these artists, that darkly sinister spirit lurking within, which is said to be represented in this show. Or is it some sort of a hoax? Would the artists rank suitably with the coiners of inexplicable verse who assemble their chop-suey sequences of words and depend on the critics to explain them?

This thought has just occurred to me: Two razor blades took my grandmother's milkman for a walk and ate a telephone with a Borsalino and three-pennyworth of leather washers and tram tickets with a Heinkel. I have set these words down regardless of their sense; should I be so presumptuous as to call them profound prose, fit for the admiration of all posterity?

Mind you, there were plenty of others who were prepared to do battle for the modern form.

Letters, Loudon Sainthill. Australia is now old enough to be giving to as well as taking from present-day European painting, and there are the artists who, in speaking for themselves, have a lot to give, as, for instance, Dobell, Lawlor, and Friend, and many others. The real progress the Gallery should make is in bringing forward by their official recognition the best work of the Australian contemporaries.

What a sign of progress it would be to find the Gallery trustees had cleared one room of the bushland bleaknesses now on view for nearly half a century, to the cellar, and hung in their stead an acquired collection of our own contemporary art. In their younger days, as well as in their maturer years, it seems the Gallery assisted such artists as Streeton and Hinton when they were more contemporary than they are today. Why not the same for the younger artists of today, whose battle for existence is an equally difficult one?

Re-hang the European masterpieces for the duration and where will we be at the end of that time? Still the same lifeless gallery, still no hope of our creative painting speaking its language in the galleries of the world.

Letters, John Reed, Secretary, C A Society, Melbourne. Inevitably, the reactionaries have sought the columns of the press to vent their hatred of anything that does not conform to accepted standards, and inevitably, too, there appears much semi-tolerant patronising criticism.

Contemporary art is accepted and acclaimed everywhere in the world except in Australia, and now the record attendances at the Melbourne and Sydney Exhibitions are showing that the public really wants to see it and know about it. Of course the Public Galleries completely ignore this public feeling, and will continue to do so until they are made to do otherwise. That time is coming very soon.

Then there is this simple Letter explaining it all to the miners back home.

Letters, R Alain. Art is conditioned by the style and the manner of thinking of an epoch. It is recognised that we are passing through what is **the first major crisis of our civilisation**; it is a period of change, of transition, of disintegration, and the aim of painters is to symbolise that disintegration in an integrated work of art. It is not decadence, as is popularly imagined, but the conscientious application of artists, writers, musicians, to the interpretation of their age.

Understanding of art only comes through the education of the eyes in their approach to the medium. Without a thorough knowledge of the trends from Seurat to Picasso that lead up to surrealism, that movement cannot be comprehended; but moreover, an evasion of surrealism and its implications is to limit understanding of that art of tomorrow which must evolve from it. For artists will continue to experiment, and it is the layman's misfortune if he will stand still, cutting himself adrift from the impregnation of new ideas and stimuli.

Comment. I am pleased we got that all sorted out. This correspondence started on October 2nd, and was still going over a month later. Its focus gradually shifted from the art itself, to the artists and the galleries, then critics, and the purveyors and promoters of art. It ended with accusations against Jewish art dealers in Sydney who were said to be artificially raising the price of all art above its natural level.

SILLY MEMORIES

People in 1940 hummed a lot. Women in the house, or men in the yard, hummed as they worked. Some even sang a few bars as they cooked in the kitchen or swept the house.

Local concerts in church halls attracted many mothers who got up and sang a tune. They were not at all good, but were never daunted, and ready to sing again next week. Men came on to the stage and yodeled, or played the gum leaf. The local shoe-maker was always there playing his accordian, and the little Scot wreaked his bag-pipes terror.

Boys and men in the streets whistled. Some of them were on tune, some could extend their repertoire to imitating bird calls. But they whistled. Patriotic songs, love songs, sometimes even church hymns.

Eighty years later, we have lost all this. We are a silent lot. Even the Postman is silent. The baker no longer stamps to the back door shouting "Baker", and the butcher and iceman have gone too,

Of course we **do** have substitute noise makers. Created by so-called musicians with all their falsettos and shouting. But, not for me. I like old-fashioned noises.

WHAT'S ON IN GREYHOUND CIRCLES?

Letters, J Smith, Concord Greyhound Club. In the past two years since the new training regulations were introduced, the NCA has received many letters from different councils expressing satisfaction at the vast improvement noticed in the conduct of greyhound training.

The two biggest causes for complaint – exercising dogs on footpaths and in parks – have been eliminated. If the Local Government Act is amended it would place the greyhounds at the mercy of a council composed of "wowsers" or men who would benefit by the suppression of dog racing, and this would be decidedly against the British principle of giving everyone "a fair go."

The man who is careful and considerate in his training activities should not be made to suffer for the actions of others.

NOVEMBER: ITALY JOINS THE PARTY

For London, and Britain, the first half of the month was a great relief. Not that bombing had ceased, but it dropped away to shorter and fewer raids, and sometimes London missed out altogether. So, it was still worrying, and full of danger, but better than before.

In mid-November, things again changed suddenly, when Hitler's bomber adopted a new policy. Instead of bombing London to spread terror, it moved into the smaller cities and struck at industrial targets in massive raids. The first such target was Coventry. **Lord Haw Haw weighed in** with this little gloat on November 22nd.

> Coventry is, as you might know, the most important place in England for the manufacture of aeroplane motors and such like. One bright night about 500 German aeroplanes flew over Coventry. They dropped about 1,000,000 lbs. of bombs. If you have any imagination at all you can imagine what kind of a hell they let loose in Coventry that night. Swedish and American papers say that nothing has happened that can be used as a comparison.

> It was formidable, the worst hell that mankind can imagine. And that went on almost the whole night through. When dawn came there was nothing left but one pile of rubbish. The factories were gone altogether. Coventry will manufacture no more engines for months and months to come. It was the heaviest blow for British industry. Even Americans express their doubts after Coventry, as to whether England can last much longer.

As the month progressed, similar damaging attacks were launched on cities such as Liverpool, and the Midlands, though the damage was often limited by the increasingly foggy weather. Another sore point for the British was that submarine attacks were once again on the increase. Some of these were launched from the coastal ports of France, and this stirred up more anti-French feeling.

But others were operating near the coast of Eire, and these were attacking shipping vessels coming up from Africa, and across the Atlantic, including America. Eire had declared its neutrality in the War, and was determined not to make itself a target by siding with the British. So she would not let the British use her western ports as a base for their anti-submarine craft. But there were expectations in many quarters that she could give some sort of support, and these sparked a lively correspondence even in Australia's *SMH*.

> **Letters, H Cotter.** Once again the old differences between England and Ireland have been thrust into the foreground, this time in relation to the question of the use of the ports of Eire for purposes of combating the U-boat menace.
>
> The Government of Mr de Valera is observing an attitude of strict neutrality, obviously the wisest course for a small independent nation of some three millions of people. The use of Eire's ports by any belligerent Power would render Eire liable to immediate attack. Who wishes to see the terrain of yet another small nation become a shambles? The "most distressful country" has had her full share of war and murder.
>
> **Letters, T Ryan.** H Cotter overlooks in the Anglo-Irish question a war situation that gravely affects

the British Empire. According to Mr Churchill, the German U-boat menace is now greater than the menace of air raids. Experts agree that this danger would disappear if Britain had access to certain Irish ports as naval bases. Mr de Valera, however, deliberately refuses to allow this in order to preserve Eire from German attack. But the means of ensuring this immunity facilitate U-boat operations against British shipping, and must, unless checked, increasingly intensify this menace to Britain, although, perhaps, not designed to be so.

Eire's neutrality which closes valuable strategic coastal bases to Britain is, therefore, a powerful aid to Germany. The grim truth of this is revealed in the cable news that Eire's present policy means the loss every day of British, Irish, Canadian and Australian lives. Her refusal, moreover, to observe a black-out provides nightly beacons for German air raiders. Does not, therefore, Eire's neutrality in view of its grave detriment to Great Britain create a war situation that cannot but occasion increasing concern and resentment throughout Britain?

Letter, Irish-Australian. Let Mr Cotter tell us what use will be Mr de Valera's righteous protestations if Hitler should decide to take over Eire as a base to launch his murderous attacks on Britain. We would then find this self-same Mr de Valera crying aloud for British aid to ward off the threat of aggression. Yet today he brusquely refuses Britain any measure of co-operation while living as a free nation, economically and physically, only by the power and might of an unconquered England.

THE TIMES SUMS UP AT NOVEMBER'S END

This is a war of ups and downs, not only in the fortunes of fighting, but also in our feelings about it. At the outset, we were all strung up to endure the worst immediately. Black-out precautions, urgent instructions about gas-masks, arrangements for dealing with casualties and wreckage, all looked to dreadful happenings prompt and widespread. So far as we at home were concerned, nothing very remarkable seemed to happen.

As the months dragged on the stern resolve to do or die tailed off into a resigned sort of acquiescence, void, except for an unanalysed belief in ultimate victory, of any very definite anticipation of what was still to come. Flanders, France, and the threat of invasion changed all that. Civilians, no less than soldiers, once more stood to arms and faced the obvious possibilities with high courage and stout hearts.

The intensive bombing of London deepened and hardened that steely mood. The first shock of that new access of frightfulness was weeks ago. Once more the crest of the wave of renewed violence seems to have passed, and we are left in its trough facing the problem of continuing into the dark days ahead the spirit of resistance to the evil thing. A different brand of courage is wanted for the ding-dong of a prolonged and temporarily indeterminate warfare.

All our reserves of the quieter brand of courage will be needed in the winter moths before us. The extremes of danger and excitement may well flare up again at times. If so, they will be met with the same confident defiance as before. But almost certainly there will be long weeks and months of less spectacular nibbling and nagging at our power of resistance and our firmness of mind.

That will be the time in which a quiet faith in a righteous cause, and a calm reliance on the capacity of ordinary men and women to endure in it, will prove themselves no less potent instruments of victory than flaming courage and bright bravery in arms. The impatient and the impetuous may feel that they are feebly sitting still; but the truth will be that, in doing so, "they also serve who only stand and wait."

Comment. Very flowery, but still a good summary of how Britain felt amidst its many ruins and many-more hopes.

ITALY IN THE NEWS

Mussolini's Italy was suddenly in the headlines. **Firstly**, she had a good, large and modern navy. Furthermore, she and her island of Sicily were stuck in the middle of the Mediterranean, and were ideally placed to harass shipping going to the Suez Canal. Since she had formally joined Germany a few months earlier, she had kept her navy at home, and just darted out a few times a week to attack various fleets and vessels opportunistically. In the scheme of things, she was not causing much damage, but she remained potentially a major problem for the British.

But on November 14th, half that problem went away. Or rather, it went down. Because on that day, the British Med fleet cornered much of the Italian Navy, and at the Battle of Taranto, sank about half of it. The clue to victory here was the aeroplanes launched from the aircraft carrier Illustrious. They were old and decrepit, but they caught the Italians by surprise, and did the job well. This was the proof the world needed of the efficacy of strike planes attacking from carriers, and served as **the model a year later for Pearl Harbour.**

Secondly. So, Italy made the front-pages because of the Taranto naval defeat. Then, she stayed on the front-pages because her adventure on land in Greece had blown up in her face. The Greeks, aided somewhat by Britain, had mustered their forces, and turned back the initial thrusts of the Italians, and instead, by the end of November, were chasing them back home across Albania. Il Duce's dreams of mighty military conquests were evaporating, and a frustrated Hitler was waiting anxiously for a signal to intervene.

Thirdly. If you look at the map you will see that Egypt and the Suez Canal are at the Eastern end of the Med, and that Libya is adjacent. So, if the Axis powers wanted to capture the Canal, they had to take Egypt via the Italian colony of Libya. Over the previous month, Italian troops had been slowly and spasmodically advancing from Libya into Egypt, and starting to menace Cairo and Alexandria in a half-hearted way. But, jumping ahead now to mid-December, and early January, the desert torpor was shattered by a sudden counter-attack by the British that saw Australian troops win a grand victory near the border of Libya at Sidi Barrani. Then a few weeks later, they had another win at Bardia, now on Libyan soil.

In these two encounters, only 130 Australians were killed, but **amazingly they took over 40,000 Italian prisoners**. After that, these fine troops went from strength to strength across Libya, **stopping only when they were called off by Churchill, and re-deployed, only to suffer calamitous defeats in Greece and then Crete.**

But to sum up Italian involvements at the end of the year, let me just say that Mussolini's Christmas would not have been all that jolly.

THE POSITION OF ALIENS IN OZ

Letters, Austrian, Brighton-le-Sands. A few days ago I received a postcard from the Radio Inspector's office reminding me of the impending expiration of my licence, and asking whether I wanted same renewed. I answered this card in the affirmative, stating at the same time that I was an alien (Austrian). The reply to my letter arrived without delay, intimating that, **being an unnaturalised subject of an enemy country I was to be denied the right to possess a broadcast listener's licence.**

After Hitler invaded Austria, life there seemed unbearable, and, like thousands of others, I applied for immigration into Australia. Classifying Austrian refugees as subjects of an enemy country appears to me as misrepresentation of facts. My mother was, until her marriage, a British subject, my father a Czecho-Slovakian, and we children became Austrians by birth. I always had a boundless predilection for all that was English.

When entry into Australia was granted to me, I felt very happy indeed, and the landing permit appeared to me like a contract between my new home country and me. The obligations this contract placed on me were kept by me to the letter. I rarely missed an occasion to prove my loyalty to Australia in a practical way, and no questions as to my status were asked, or objections made then. It is my firm belief that the obligations of this contract ought to be kept by both parties. It is only fairness I ask for.

Letters, Alien Couple, Maroubra. May I ask for what reason **the NSW Government has refused to teach English to adult refugees?** In this beach suburb, there are dozens of German and Austrian families, many have been here for a decade. Some of them are recent refugees. But every one of them has a hatred of Hitler and all he stands for. They did not come to Australia because they liked living under Nazism. They did not come here, with their children, so that they could send photos of the Harbour Bridge back to the Fatherland. They came here, and stayed here, because this land would give them an opportunity to live and bring up their children in a free and non-fearful society.

When we arrived here, we entered into a variety of arrangements under varying circumstance that made us promise to be loyal to this country. We promised to be good citizens. On the other hand, Australia promised us that we would be respected and treated fairly. But I cannot see what is fair about cutting off English classes to parents. How else can we learn the language? How else can we mix in society? How else can we earn a living here without the language?

There is nothing fair about this new rule. It does not respect us. It says that we are terrible people, and not worthy of the help that was promised us.

Comment one. The position of aliens, and refugees, and foreign nationals still remained completely unresolved. Every jurisdiction had its own rules and definitions. The States, the Commonwealth, the Courts, the police, the Army, a dozen Government Departments, all had their own views. A Mr Posetti from Corrimal, wrote that he had been here thirty years, and in recent months had been interned twice, and released twice, by four different agencies. But, he added, in **WWI** he had been a welcome guest because then Italy was on our side. What, he asked, had he done wrong to be interned now?

Comment two. It was not all bad news on this front. The Minister for the Army, Mr Spender, announced today that, in future, selected aliens would be permitted to offer for enlistment. This excluded persons from Germany. He said that persons of unambiguous loyalty to the cause for which the Empire is fighting would be eligible. He did not explain how they would define or determine "unambiguous loyalty."

Despite this ray of sanity, the whole matter remained a complete mess.

THE MELBOURNE CUP

Letters, Linda Littlejohn. I turned on the radio early this morning and by chance heard a commentator speaking on the forthcoming Melbourne race meeting. He concluded his remarks with these words: "This should be a record meeting, and we can rest assured that Flemington will not let us down." I do hope that those brave folk in England, who at present are losing their homes, their business, their family and friends, picked up that splendid thought and that our army, navy, and air force, wherever they be, also heard it, for they will be glad to know that Flemington is not letting them down.

The commentator seems very sure of his belief, but many of us would like to know how such a remark can be justified at this the most challenging moment in our history.

Letters, J Burwood. Undoubtedly in offices, factories, clubs, etc., countless sweepstakes will be arranged as in the past. Under present circumstances, I think that patriotic funds should benefit from these sweepstakes, and I suggest that when they are organised it be stated that so much will be devoted to the office Comforts Fund, the Lord Mayor's Fund, the Red Cross, or whatever patriotic fund is chosen by the organisers.

Letters, G Crivelli. In seeking a justification for racing comments in time of crisis, Mrs Littlejohn could do no better than turn to "those brave folk in England". Did they not set us the example of refusing to allow the most disastrous of calamities to shake their cool indifference to the Hun? At the very moment when France was in her death agonies, the English Derby was run as usual, attracting thousands of people. The results of the Derby and the fall of Paris appeared side by side on news hoardings. I think, therefore, if English listeners do chance to pick up stray comments on Australian racing, they will acknowledge that races can still be held while every aid is being given to the war effort.

Letters, J Duncan. I wish to state that there are millions of loyal Australians whose spirit must be kept up by healthy recreation and amusement. If the war effort is to be maintained and the sporting fraternity are to continue to give both in money and services, no unjust discrimination of the people's rights or choice of recreation, amusement, or sport should be tolerated. In Australia, the races are patronised by thousands of worthy citizens, who, with many owners and trainers, have contributed very generously in money and services toward the war effort.

Letters, A Eather. I protest against race meetings in a time of crisis. Are the crowded race-courses in Australia our answer to Mr Churchill's call to the Empire, when he said "Come, then! Let us to the task – to the battle, and the toil. There is not a week – nor a day – nor an hour to be lost." They who argue that it is vital for people to have racing as recreation at such a time remind one of the ostrich with his head in the sand.

Letters, Punter. There are all sorts of people who are seizing on the War to try to mould the world into the shape they want it. If you don't like horse-racing, object to it because of the War. If you do not like dancing, point out how immoral it is and that it interferes with the serious business of the War. Football matches, drinking in pubs, driving on Sundays, women's photos in magazines, all lessen our war effort, we are told.

Of course it is all tommy rot. These people are always against these things and are just using the War as another way to push their own barrows. Let me ask them, are we supposed to be toiling for the war effort 24 hours a day? I could keep that up for about a day. If I go to the races on a Saturday, and have a day of Biblical rest on a Sunday, I go to work refreshed on a Monday and do a better week's work than any wowser who spends her time wallowing in the agonies of her own mind.

VIEWS OF SOME CLERGY

Letters, F Jeater. Intemperance, sexual vice, gambling, lack of Sunday observance, and other social or moral questions are undoubtedly evils that the Church should fight, but they are always with us, war or no war, and although they may to some extent retard our war efforts, yet we must ever recognise that the present urgent need is to win the war.

Our clergy should give up all talk about pacifism and turning the other cheek. They should be more emphatic in emphasising that we are battling for truth and righteousness and to keep the door open for all individual and social improvement, and should encourage the nation and individuals to make all sacrifices of life and material wealth that are necessary for victory. By sounding this more positive note they would keep the objective of the war on high spiritual levels, improve the morale of the nation, and bring back many of the people into their churches.

OTHER LETTERS

Letters, C Forrest, Muswellbrook P and C. The children of Muswellbrook are keen on raising funds to purchase for the nation a Spitfire warplane. To do this about 5,000 Pounds has to be raised.

These enthusiastic little workers have already funds to the extent of 18 Pounds, and they have organised a carnival for the 22nd instant, when they hope to reach their 50 Pound objective.

They would like to know of, say, 100 New South Wales towns which would, through children's committees, aim at raising 50 Pounds from each town for the **purpose of purchasing a Spitfire warplane for the nation**.

Letters, J McNamara. Dr Walker, in his "War-time Economics," has rightly pointed out that, in war-time, no Government should be forced into the ridiculous position of competing with private enterprise for men, materials, and money.

I have done a lot of hard thinking on the question of Christmas shopping this year. Some items

I have discarded as completely frivolous. The money I will save there will be used to buy war saving certificates and war saving stamps as Christmas presents for my family.

Letters, A Pain. One needs to be very deaf not to **hear of troop movements and war activities almost daily**. Today, over the radio, **gossipers** are called "fools or criminals". Apparently, the campaign is to be stronger, but will it be any more effective? This problem of inducing people to hoard these military secrets may be one of psychology.

For instance, instead of broadcasting such disparaging epithets as "gossips, fools, and criminals", would it be more successful to invite listeners to "join the silent service?"

VERA LYNN

Vera was a singer who emerged in 1940 as the spokes-singer for Britain. Her plaintive songs talking of the pains of war, and separation from loved ones, caught the nostalgia of the nation, and earned her the title of "the Nation's Sweetheart."

To me, In Australia, she epitomised the courage of the nation. Her singing was carried non-stop by the wireless, and pulled at the heartstrings constantly. My mother always got tearful when Vera sang "and Willy will go to sleep, in his own little room once more"

Even today, when I am singing in the shower, if I stray onto Vera's songs, when I inevitably come to *Blue Birds* over Dover, I choke and pause for a minute before I finish.

It's funny how old memories come back over the years.

DECEMBER: THE END OF A TOUGH YEAR

How was Britain coping? This **news item** gives us another view of the embattled nation.

Although probably at least 1,000,000 women and children and aged and infirm people have gone from London, a regrettably high number remain, even in the most heavily bombed areas. Indeed, it is common to see small boys at play in the bigger craters. An official estimate puts the number of children still in London at nearly 300,000.

The Government are making a fresh attempt to get more women and children away, and investigations, which I have made, suggest that they would be more likely to succeed if the Ministry of Health were to review and improve the arrangements for those who have left London behind.

The population of one town in the Home Counties has increased from 100,000 by nearly half as many again. Fifty thousand people have poured in, and still they come. The town is packed, and the chance visitor has no hope of finding an hotel bedroom. The town is typical of every town and village within a radius of 50 miles of the capital.

Under present arrangements it seems to be nobody's business to make known when an area is full, or give other useful guidance of the kind to those leaving London. It is almost as if the central authorities lose interest once those who are leaving are on the train out of London. It may be pleaded that they cannot be blamed where people, without registration or prior warning, descend on a country town, but the conclusion is inescapable that the Ministry of Health should be exercising a much more thorough oversight over the whole problem **in the reception districts**. In particular, it is urged by residents of rural areas who are struggling hard to place people where only small cottages exist, the Ministry should make it clear that it may not always be possible to billet all the members of large families together.

In this – and some other districts – there are many families who in the summer, when invasion seemed possible, were sent away from towns in Kent for six weeks. Since then bombing of their home towns has prompted the authorities to keep them here longer. Accordingly, these people, with the days growing colder, are still here with nothing but thin summer clothes.

The article went on to say that there was a shortage of beds. Even when people got a roof over their heads, there were just no beds. There were none in the shops, and anyone who had previously had a spare, had already given it up for the War Effort. Even pots and pans and other household utensils were in great scarcity, because all spare ones had been donated to drives for scrap aluminium and steel.

In short, for the displaced Londoner, and there were millions of them, things were often very tough.

WHAT OF BRITAIN'S FUTURE?

Britain had seen a terrible military year. It started when gallant, but friendless, Finland was defeated by the Russians, and continued with the conquest of Norway, and the retreat of the British with their tails between their legs. Only a few months later, there was the fall of Luxemburg, Denmark and Holland, and the losing battles in Belgium. Then came the ignominy of Dunkirk, topped off by the defeat of France, and its armistice and neutrality with the Germans. After that followed the Battle of Britain and the Blitz, and the very real fear of invasion. If someone told a story about all this, or wrote it into a novel, I at least would dismiss it as fanciful rubbish, just another version of science fiction. But it was true. Incredible as it seems, it did happen. And equally incredible, the nation survived and was still kicking. Amazing.

It was not all bad. By the end, Britain could say with great satisfaction that the RAF had achieved real and lasting victories in and around Britain, and had let Germany know that she was a real threat to its territory. She had come from a mile behind in submarine warfare, and was slowly getting on top there. And her navy continued to rule the waves, with the occasional mishap.

From the point of view of the population, bombings in Britain were a lot fewer than in the previous months. In December, there were a number of two-night periods without any bombings. These were generally followed by a big raid on a regional centre, like Manchester, but bombings were much more piecemeal than before. Everyone could see that there was no real reason for them to continue indefinitely; **they would stop someday**.

German subs were still seen to be taking a big toll, but it seemed that they were being cornered a bit more. The Air Force was fighting for its life over Britain and Europe, but the winter weather brought a merciful relief. Comfortingly, it appeared to be gradually winning, and improving its position, as more planes were imported from America, and more pilots came in from the Empire Training Scheme.

Everyone was greatly relieved that the threat of invasion seemed to be gone. It was a great consolation that fighting on the ground was now moving away from Britain, and towards the shores of Tripoli and Egypt and the like. Also, that the participants now included large numbers of Australians, New Zealanders, and Indians. It seemed that Britain had lost one ally, France, but at this critical time, the Empire had stepped up as a better replacement.

But the biggest worry was still nagging at the populace every day. **The menfolk remained at great risk.** Every day, sailors, airmen, soldiers, merchant men, submariners, and others, were all being killed and maimed. The tragedy of this was ever-haunting, ongoing, touching everyone in the nation. If military prospects were a bit brighter, then that was good. But for the people at home, there could be no peace of mind until their own loved ones were safely back on British soil.

OZ POLITICS ON THE NOSE

The end of the year came at a good time for Federal parliamentarians. They had just about done all the tricks they could muster, and needed a spell of two months to think things out. In December, they dithered and dallied. Would they form a single, National Government? No way. But, suppose they did, could they agree on who should lead it? No way. Could they pull together and agree on policies in preparation for war? Not on your life.

Cries for unity of purpose came from everywhere.

Letters, L Clunies Ross, University of Sydney.
To anyone who has studied Dr Goebbels' technique, it is certain that if he considered the creation of disunity and suspicion in Australia worthy of his distinguished attention, he would play up by every means just **such class and State jealousies as are now so deplorable a feature of Australian life**. I have no doubt that those who, by word or deed, perpetuate the barriers which now divide us are, at best, unconsciously playing the part of fifth columnists and assisting the enemy. It is they, and not the aliens in our midst, who are a danger to the State.

If in the face of the perils which now confront us we are incapable of developing a new vision and purpose to animate our national life, if we are content to travel the old road with all its petty bickering between class and class or State and State, then we are false to those principles for which we allege we are fighting, and we deserve the doom which should overtake us.

Is Australia to be just another example of the failure of democracy to eliminate the faults which undermine its whole fabric, until the bombs and shells are falling amongst its women and children? It is not enough for us **to deplore the lack of idealism and moral purpose in our politicians**. It is our responsibility as men of adult stature to demonstrate our possession of those qualities which we claim they lack, and by our help and cooperation rather than ungenerous criticism so to inspire them that they too, Government and Opposition alike, shall be fired with a new zeal to work and fight not for party, class, or State, but for Australia.

Amid the general confusion, one thing stood out. That was that Menzies, who had won the election just a few months ago, was rapidly losing support from the people.

Letters, Geo Michaels. I am not a Labor supporter, but I am convinced that Australia's present leadership lacks the appeal, drive, and personality to unite the community in bonds of service. It is a form of leadership that may have been all right in the piping days of peace and prosperity. Today, however, it is deficient in the qualities of a Churchill, the power of a Smuts or the organising ability of a Mackenzie King. I pray that there will be a drastic change before it is too late. We owe it to ourselves, and above all to Britain.

Comment. Mr Michaels' sentiment was echoed over and over by people who were saying "Menzies is not a war-time leader." If he did not do something soon, he would clearly lose office. But the good thing for him at this time of year was that, then as now, half-way through the month, Australia shut down for six weeks, so he could shelve his worries for a while.

WOMEN VOLUNTEERS

Women had responded very well to the call to provide services. Numbers had enlisted in the Armed Services. Many more had volunteered for other public services, such as fire fighting and as civilian drivers for the Forces. Still more had joined in fund raising groups, and Ladies Auxiliaries that ran functions to provide benefits for the Services. These latter groups had recently come in for some criticism on the grounds that some of them were there more for social occasions than for their expressed purposes.

Letters, Alister Greer. For many months past, we have noticed a large part of the feminine population bedecked in what has seemed a multitudinous variety of uniforms. That there were official women's organisations, we knew; that women could do their part in preparation for the contingencies of war, we agreed; that many women desired to contribute their share to the national effort of preparedness, we did not doubt.

But when so many different uniforms appeared, and when many of us, after experiencing heavy military socks and boots, were confronted with feminine uniforms which included sheer stockings, a doubt began to arise as to whether some of these organisations existed for utility or mere show. Moreover, we learned that these bodies of zealous women were so patriotic that they provided their own uniforms, at a cost ranging from 5 Pounds upwards; which gave rise to the speculation that perhaps this money might have been put to more patriotic use by investment in War Savings Certificates.

Now has come the request for volunteers to fill ARP positions. This is a work which demands real service in the face of real danger; work which requires high courage, with patriotism and the desire to serve in the highest degree. Unfortunately, there are not any pretty uniforms to be secured, and in view of this fact the dearth of women ARP volunteers seems to assume a significant aspect.

If the enrolment in the many women's organizations is motivated by a genuine desire to serve, the apathy shown towards ARP can only be classed as coincidental. Otherwise it must surely appear as a timely exposure of much humbug and play-acting, involving time, energy, and money, which could surely be put to better use.

Letters, Nil Desperandum. The opposition and disinterest displayed by citizens is most disheartening to those who were patriotic enough to join up and be trained under the National Emergency Services and give up most of their spare time to study and train for the protection of the very people who were holding the whole organisation up to "ridicule".

This is not a women's organisation, we are merely an auxiliary, and, as such were not allowed to wear a distinguishing uniform, and there is not any doubt that when uniformed units of women's organisation sprang up like mushrooms, we lost many of our members for the sake of a uniform. For eighteen months we have been preparing for any emergency, "unheralded and unsung" – no publicity, no uniform, only a cotton working dress; and now, after all our hard work, we find "untrained" and partially trained women coming out in lavish uniforms costing anything between 5 Pounds and 6 Pounds, making the State Government organisation women look like "poor relations". Consequently, we have been forced into a uniform – just plain, not glamorous

– against our wishes, but should the bombs ever fall our working dress will be well to the fore.

Letters, P Cain. I am a member of a voluntary organisation who are collecting money for our boys overseas. We are all quite well-off, but strangely, we seem to care for them as much as do the poor working class.

We work at our fund raising just as hard as those poverty-stricken saints who are not in uniform, but we like the glamour that uniforms provide. Is there any good reason why we cannot indulge ourselves these? They only cost six Pounds, and make us feel good, and I can tell you, they help to keep our volunteers. To talk about buying war certificates with the money is just plain silly. What difference would a few hundred pounds make?

The fact is that we are out and doing our bit. We do it our way, and according to our means. If everyone would do the same, including the poverty-stricken saints, this country would be much better off.

GERMANS ON OUR SHORES

Early in December, a German mother ship and a couple of small frigates sailed along the south coast of Australia, dropping mines in Bass Straight. It moved to New Zealand, and out into the South Pacific. Shortly after that, two Oz tramp ships struck mines in the Straight, and sank. Then a few more ships were sunk off New Zealand, and finally the phosphate loading wharfs at Nauru were shelled on Christmas Day.

It started to occur to people that perhaps war could invade our shores, and that we should not just be intent on aiding Britain, but maybe we should start to prepare for attacks here as well. Words of caution started to appear in the Press.

Letters, George Fitzpatrick. The Japanese Government announces that, through the Japanese Broadcasting Corporation, a special news service will be directed to Australia from January next. The Japs want to present their point of view to Australians in our language.

What is being done to present the Australian point of view, in Japanese, to the people of Japan through a station directed to Japan? Surely this unique opportunity will not be overlooked.

Letters, Cowper, FRAIA, Sydney. Mr Thomas F Rose, FRCS, is correct when he suggests that "the authorities in Sydney should benefit from the experience of London and build permanent, deep bomb-proof shelters." In Sydney it is suggested by the authorities that the underground railway tunnels be used as deep shelters, but this would not accommodate more than 25 per cent of the population of this city. We need to think deeply about this.

Comment. A year from now, we would be at war with Japan, and under serious threat of invasion. At the moment though, most people were so fascinated by the European War that they gave little thought to what was happening in Asia. There were some politicians in the Labor Party, John Curtin in particular, who were becoming quickly aware of this, but most people didn't worry about it. Looking back, it appears obvious that the conduct of

Japan, and of America, in this period made it likely that a Pacific War would be fought, but such an idea was at the moment foreign to us, and in no way interfered with Christmas festivities in Oz.

SUMMING UP 1940 IN OZ

Needless to say, the War in Britain had caused a great effect on Australia. In one sense, this is very strange. After all, it was 12,000 miles away from Australia, the planes that were bombing London could not get anywhere near us, the subs and ships scarcely visited our waters, and no one was going to ship off armies just to conquer Tasmania. So, you could argue that we were thoroughly insulated, and that we would be advised to keep out it. Perhaps we, like America, should seek economic bliss by just supplying war materials.

But there was never a thought of doing this. Australia was living, day by day, the whole British experience. Our loyalty to the Empire and to the Crown were unquestioned, and we suffered and rejoiced in the same breath as the British.

As part of this, over 1940, our whole society had been militarised. Not to the same extent as the British, but it was still very obvious. Enlistments, rationing of petrol, training camps, men in uniform, munitions factories, restrictions on photography, requisitions of properties, internment of aliens. On and on goes the list. Everyone talked all the time about matters military. **Young schoolboys dreamed of them.**

As for the general population, it was frustrated. It wanted to help Britain in any way possible and practical. We had mustered soldiers and airmen, and sent them off. It was obvious that we could do more, much more. But all Governments across the nation were so caught up in their internal politics, in their own factional squabbles, in plain old-fashioned politicking for survival, that they were almost useless in the fast-moving world they were then in. So frustration was the sentiment of the day.

Apart from that, the pre-occupation with Britain made us lose track of developments in Asia and Japan. Next year, this would come home to haunt us, because next year we would see the start of **our own replay of the British experience**. And then, it would be **our own shores that would be threatened**.

So, that means I must conclude on a solemn note. I can look at Australia at the end of 1940, and say that things weren't too bad. Granted we had our military in danger overseas, and we had just been hit with an enormous tax increases. Things, though, were not too bad. But if I have a quick glance ahead, I can see that the following three years for Australia will be the toughest that it had ever faced, or would ever face, probably.

Still, in the long run, I can see that **the blue birds did ultimately return to Dover**, so perhaps I can lighten up a bit.

OTHER BOOKS IN THIS SERIES

In 1939, Hitler bullied Europe, he took over a few countries, and he bamboozled the Brits. By the end of the year, most of Europe ganged up on him, and a phony war had millions of men idling in trenches eating their Christmas turkeys. Back in Oz, the drunkometer was breathlessly awaited, pigeon pies were on the nose, our military canteens were sometimes wet and sometimes dry. Nasho for young men was back, Sinatra led his bobby-soxers, and girls of all ages swooned for crooner Bing

In 1949, the Reds in China could rest from their Long March, and the Reds in Australia took a battering in the pits. The rabbits ruled the paddocks, and some Churches suffered from outbreaks of dirty dancing and housie. Immigration Minister Calwell crudely enforced the White Australia Policy, so that huge crowds on the beaches were nervous about getting a tan. There was plenty of petrol for motorists in NZ and Britain, but not here, so Bob Menzies cruised to another election win over Labor.

Birthday and Chrissi gifts for Mum and Dad and Aunt and Uncle and cousins and family and friends and work and everyone else.

Don't forget a good read and chuckle for yourself

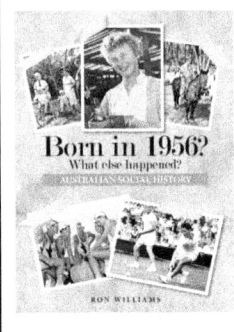

In 1956, the first big issue was the Suez crisis, which put our own Bob Menzies on the world stage, but he got no applause. Quite the opposite. TV was turned on in time for the Melbourne Olympics, where our cover girl won gold. Sydney also saw them but only as replays. Hungary was invaded and the Iron Curtain got a lot thicker. There was much concern about cruelty to sharks, and the horrors of country pubs persisted.

In 1958, the Christian brothers bought a pub and raffled it; some clergy thought that Christ would not be pleased. Circuses were losing animals at a great rate. Officials were in hot water because the Queen Mother wasn't given a sun shade; it didn't worry the lined-up school children, they just fainted as normal. School milk was hot news, bread home deliveries were under fire. The RSPCA was killing dogs in a gas chamber. A tribe pointed the bone at Albert Namatjira; he died soon after.

These books are available at boombooks.biz

Soft covers for each of the years from 1939 to 1970

Hard covers for 1939, 1949, 1959, 1969, and 1958

And also for 1940, 1950, 1960, and 1970

www.ingramcontent.com/pod-product-compliance
Lightning Source LLC
Chambersburg PA
CBHW070729020526
44107CB00077B/2217